Copyright © 2017
Jenny Forrester

Library of Congress
Cataloging-in-Publication Data

Hawthorne Books
& Literary Arts

The Library of Congress control number is LCCN 2016041304

9   2201 Northeast 23rd Avenue
8   3rd Floor
7   Portland, Oregon 97212
6   hawthornebooks.com
5   *Form*:
4   Sibley House
3
2   Printed in China
1   Set in Paperback

For Chiara
and
in loving memory of Judy Marshall

Narrow River, Wide Sky

A Memoir
Jenny Forrester

HAWTHORNE BOOKS & LITERARY ARTS
Portland, Oregon | MMXVII

Contents

MEMORY IS A TRICKY THING, BUT MEMOIR IS STRAIGHT-forward – I gathered memories to create a narrative arc that seeks to tell The Truth. As the writer of this book, I took liberties with my memories and the timeline of events to create a narrative. Some names have been changed, but most haven't. Identities are the ones I've projected onto the various characters of my life's story. If anyone recognizes themselves in this story, they would do well to remember that I'm using them in this way and that their lives are much bigger than any one story could contain.

NARROW RIVER, WIDE SKY

I. Children of a Narrow River

1. The Narrow River

MY BROTHER AND I STOOD NEAR THE TOP OF A SLOPING western Colorado cemetery, among the ghosts of pioneers with their upright gravestones on one side and the more recent ghosts on the other, their earthen beds marked with the metal stakes of the impoverished, considering where we should bury our mother, taken from us, suddenly. We were in our twenties and not ready, not that anyone ever is. Our sweet mother. Her skin of rose cream and cold, calloused hands, her warm, soft heart, a cup of tea in a coffee place.

Brian pointed toward Hard Scrabble Mountain away from the cream coffee-colored hills above the Eagle River. We looked at it from her future perspective, and we didn't like the narrowness of it. She liked expanses, the wider view. She'd suffered narrowness long enough.

He walked to another spot and said, "This is good. She can see New York Mountain from here." He turned his back – armored, facing away up over what most people would call mountains, being born children at high altitude.

"I don't know if this is the place." I wanted more time to make the right decision, permanent as it was.

The grave digger, awaiting our decision for our mother's resting place, moved from foot to foot, his strong arms across his wide chest and said, "There's no room for anyone beside her."

"She wasn't married," we said, too much at once.

He grimaced in frustration at our ignorance about the burial of kin and said, "But you two can never be buried with her. There's no space for you as a family."

"What if she's alone," I said as an unanswerable question.

"It's here, Jenny. This is where she has to be buried."

Raised to be polite, our arguments were subtle. Submerged. Molten like the landscape – constant pressure, yet inseparably bound.

Brian had always cherished authority, and I'd come to question it, but convinced by Brian and their shared underlying belief in the act of certainty, the man said, "I'll get the backhoe."

I'd slept in Mom's bed the night before to be near her, to keep something of her – the scent of roses and tea and skin-softening night cream – small things become everything when someone dies.

I read her journals. Forgive me. I know. I did.

She wrote this about Thanksgiving, her last one, "At dinner, Jenny told me a story about a panther that lost her paw when she put it through a fence at a wildlife sanctuary. The owners thought the panther should've known better than to stick her paw in where the lions were feeding. Can't stop thinking about that poor panther. I've been so sad about it. I hope this is my last Thanksgiving."

She'd raised us with a depth of optimism that used to annoy me, having been a sensitive child. Her words laid hard on that page. She wrote other things, too, that I hadn't known or imagined resided in her.

I shared the faith Brian had in the landscape to provide solace and sanctuary, but I worried about the ghosts and demons she'd have to navigate on her own because she'd been fighting them all her life. When would she have peace?

How could I live without her, and how could I live with myself? I'd told my mother a sad story that made her wish for death on a page of her private thoughts.

AS CHILDREN, WE'D lived on two acres not many miles from the cemetery just below where a creek flowed into the narrow river from the high mountains to the south and spread out into the grassy pasture where the rosehips grew. In the spring, it was all water and tall grass. Chicks grew from chickhood to chickenhood and were beheaded, and Mom planted the garden on the drier side of the property, fenced off from domesticated and wild goats alike.

We watched goats drop their newborn babies encased in the sac their mothers would later eat to sustain themselves. Some babies never got up, while others stood and shook, licked clean, ready to run from mountain lions or bears or from our father and mother or from us.

At five years old, I had the job of caring for a mother hen and her three chicks separated from the flock in their own coop on the outside of the big barn. One morning, I found the hen but none of her chicks standing in the high elevation sunshine behind the wire. I saw a flash of black and white and a long, feathered tail as a magpie flew over and dropped a yellow chick's body, whole but empty, at my feet and then landed on the livestock gate and yelled in its magpie tongue. Then I found a little spine, a foot, a tiny head, and a body unrelated to that head among the round stones in the packed dirt of the chicken yard.

I cried and ran into the house.

"The magpies got my babies." I sought justice or understanding or direction at my father's feet propped up on the couch, football on the television in the background.

Dad got up and grabbed his gun. He shot magpies all morning. My little brother and I hid behind furniture, running from room to room, covering our ears. Shots exploded, and Dad cursed at every magpie in their tiding before firing. There were many, and he hardly ever missed. I burst away from my fear to tell the magpies to hide, but when I got to the window just before I could send a warning to them, they fell from the branches of the trees we played in. I saw one fall from Brian's tree – head and body fell separately, at nearly the same time.

We held the grief of small animals when we had to. We felt

the freedom in sharing their small worlds in fields of wildflowers and thistles and in trees we shared with hosts of sparrows and chimes of wrens. We spent hours of our young childhoods in two trees by the road in front of the house. Brian imagined the trees as tractors, digging the ditch deeper. My tree held me, watching, listening, talking, helping Brian with his imaginary ditch when asked, but mostly he changed the world on his own, and I listened and watched and told stories.

Brian and I looked up into the mountain valley, filled with animals, as we played or rode along winding highways in the van – bighorn sheep, deer, and elk. A bobcat broke into the chicken coop during the winter and killed them all, but didn't eat any. We faulted her mostly for that. Dad shot her through the ear.

Saddened, Mom said, "Poor hens. Such good layers. That bobcat killed because it could."

"Well, that's the way with animals. No thoughts, just instincts," Dad said.

"You don't know that." She hardened and put her hands on her hips in restraint. Mom thought more of the inner lives of animals than anyone except me.

Dad said, "Oh, you're a baby," picked her up, swung her over his shoulder, and made cave-man noises until she laughed.

Mom picked up the dead bobcat. Dad took a picture of her as she smiled, wearing a blue parka, her mittens in the snow behind her. In her bare hands, she held the dead cat's neck and tail, eyes half closed, turning the color of decay. The bloodied chickens lay around her in the deep Colorado snow, the rooster with his long colorful tail, still beautiful, a scythe-like curve at her feet. Someone tanned the hide and we kept it as a decoration the way some people keep doilies on their furniture.

For a while, we had a brown-bodied, too-small-for-our-father, horse named Pegasus. Mom rode between Brian and me – Brian in front and me behind holding on to her. Peggy liked to stand on the porch, looking in the windows.

Dad, bare armed, dirt and oil covered hands, yelled, "Why's the horse always on the porch? Can't we keep her off of it?"

Mom, in the kitchen, forever turning the heavy metal separator's handle, goat milk dripping into one pail, cream into a bowl, had a different concern, "She breaks the fences. That's really the problem."

Dad considered himself to be the better fence builder, but Mom could fix and mend fences, too. Pegasus had to be fetched often running along the shoulderless highway. We wondered what she searched for.

Our father trained two lab pups to become hunting dogs, but both died on the highway – one at a time, neither growing to adulthood – the only times I saw him cry. The Benway boys and Brian often had Mercurochrome stains on their heads covering the various wounds they got playing in barns and fields. I used caution around them, played where they wouldn't wander, played with dolls so they'd leave me alone. It didn't always work because Brian, the other boys, and G.I. Joe went to war to protect America, and my dolls were the enemy. They came through with their gunfire sounds exploding between their teeth and their sweeping, pounding, and gripping fists. When G.I. Joe's army left, I cleaned up after them, and then I told on them.

Mom said, "Work it out with him," and "Seek your better angel," when I pointed to the destruction.

In the spring, Brian and his friend Eric found a bunch of kittens behind the Benway's barn. Brian brought one home. He bit her paws – her paws a pacifier. Mom dabbed Vaseline on the cat's paws when they broke open. She tsk'd and hmm'd angry mumblings, and I cried and whined about her not stopping him, but she said, "Boys will be boys, I suppose." Brian named her Crackers, like saltines. Throughout her lifetime, she'd attack at random, going for the ankles.

I told an egg-buying visitor about the cat's paws, and I remember the shocked expression, Mom's shushing, the sympathetic look from egg-buyer to the cat and to me. I reached for the stranger's hand. Saw Mom's cheeks redden. Let go of the power-less hand.

OUR WEEKDAY BABYSITTER, who taught me how to print and made pots of refried beans and took care of all the cuts on heads, wasn't available one day, but her daughter was.

We were at the Benway's house and the babysitter's daughter took me into the bathroom and told me to put my fingers in her vagina. I didn't think I heard right.

What? What? Why? No. No. No. No. No.

I remember her bigger than Mom, smaller than Dad. Solid. Sixteen. I was five. I knew she got in fights at school. In the street. Tough. We kids knew about her.

She took off her pants and underwear and stood close and grabbed my hand, held all but two fingers back and said, "Put your fingers in me." My fingers were in. She held them there.

"Smell them," she said. No. She smelled my fingers. Smell them, she said. She put my fingers to my nose. "We smell good," she said.

"Lay down," she said.

I lay down.

She kneeled over me and said, "Put your finger in me."

Time passed. So much time passed. I needed to pee. She let me.

Brian and Larry knocked on the door. I heard them laughing and running around. Something crashed. Broken. More knocking. The boys needed to pee, too. She didn't let them in.

Later, Mom said we were going to the Benway's again and Isabel would babysit.

No. No. No. No. No.

"Why?" she said.

I said, "I don't know."

I don't remember whether she babysat again or not.

The Minnesota relatives visited. Our grandfather had visited us. He walked among the thistles and goats and chickens while we showed him where the events of our lives happened – the place where I fell off the horse, the place where Brian found a big frog. The goats sniffed his shiny shoes.

Uncle John lived in a cottage behind the house for several months after he returned from Vietnam. He needed some time alone, Mom said. He'd gone to "Dog Lab," become a medic, and served two tours. He left again to Minnesota, married Aunt Barb and adopted the little boy she'd had from her first marriage, and they visited the farm. I remember he said he wanted to spank his little boy one hundred times. After he spanked the child and joined us outside by the livestock gate, he said he'd counted pretty high, but didn't get to a hundred. We'd heard a cry per strike. Mom told me not to speak about it as I stood beside her counting heart beats, blocking out the crying. I don't know how many smacks I heard.

Brian and I imagined ourselves to be pioneers because the grown men and women in our lives believed themselves to be pioneers. Our father, in particular, had a mythology he built with stories that he told at random intervals while taking breaks from fixing a truck or sitting on the back step sharpening a knife.

He told stories about eighty-pound porcupines to scare us. My brother feared nothing, he said, but I feared vampires and volcanoes and porcupines.

Dad said, "I did the first ever front flip off a ski jump in the Vail Valley." He had a sidewise smile, his eyes magnified large and round through his thick glasses.

And he said, "I'm the only one who'll ski down into the avalanche areas because I know the snow like the back of my hand. I know how it thinks." Partly true, we all knew about the landscape, having lived in it, but Mom told us to be humble when Dad talked like that. She told us nobody was smarter than snow in an avalanche. Best to stay clear. Or maybe she only said it to me. My brother has no memory of this.

Our father said, "I saved hundreds of lives. You wouldn't believe the scrapes people get into at ski resorts," and he said, "I'm a Minnesotan, a descendent of Vikings."

He hated the federal government. "That land over there," he looked across the small mountain highway, "owned by a seventy-year-old rancher, but the feds put him in jail anyway. He paid the Basque shepherds in cash only, and the feds didn't like that. He tried to explain that he had to pay them in cash because the Basques don't trust anything but cash. He told them it was their way of life, and he couldn't just change their way of life. But, they put him in jail."

According to Dad, Earth First! had it in for him and his friends – he had a friend of a friend who had to report to the police that a bomb had been planted by Earth First! on one of the newer ski runs, which cut the trees out of the mountains and reached ever further back to where the mountains turned to stone and glacier.

"Innocent Ski Patrollers coulda been killed. Those guys were out there helping people – innocent skiers."

He talked about "liberal pansies" and corrupt politicians.

He called doctors by their first names. "I'm on the ski patrol. We've worked on ski accident victims together." Mom whispered to Brian and me that it was rude to do that. "Thinks he's allowed," she breathed anger we weren't supposed to respond to and should act like we didn't hear. The navigating of parents and their rages and secrets.

Dad couldn't always work. He ruined his elbow building civilization into the Vail Valley and then ruined his knee on the ski patrol. He said, "One too many pulls of the sled, one too many heavy lifts, and one too many idiots depending on me to save him."

He told stories of crime – Old West style, his blue eyes smiling.

His racism was a twisted kind of inventive. He made up his own pejoratives, "There were these Texicans who shot another rancher right off of his horse. He made a fairly good tourniquet and got himself home."

He liked stories that put him in the same social circle as ranchers. Two acres, two thousand acres – all the same.

He told of hunting dog packs – dogs turned wild because people didn't walk them, just set them loose into the mountains at night. These dog packs, Dad said, attacked Dixon's donkey and so had to be killed.

He and Mr. Dixon went out with their rifles up into the forested mountains across the highway and up the steep trail toward Lions Head Rock.

"Those dogs started hunting us. We were out there in the dark, back to back, rifles pointed out, protecting ourselves – we had to walk like that all the way down the mountain. Dixon couldn't let it rest, though. He went back out alone and shot every last one of those dogs. People in town got upset about losing their dogs. Can you believe that? It's just like people, though – not to take care of what's theirs and then get mad over losing it."

Mom did seasonal work in Vail and in other parts of the valley in restaurants, at the Vail Mountain ticket office, at the ski school, in day care, and in the public schools. She taught English and Spanish for a while in Red Cliff, driving up toward Leadville on winding, icy roads past the red quartzite cliffs, scarred by mine tailings, older and newer. She'd learned Spanish at the University of Minnesota after falling in love with a boy who wanted to go to South America to save souls. She decided to ski instead.

Brian and I went to school in Minturn, a town made up in large part of people with Mexican ancestry, referred to by our father (and his ski patrol buddies) with words that made Mom wince and say, "Carl," with a growl under her tongue. She didn't want us using those words, she told us, "Be careful with words."

I started second grade when Brian started kindergarten.

"Take care of him," Mom said. "Make sure he gets on the right bus." I got him on the right bus and took a different one because I didn't believe we'd be on the same one. The bus driver called Mom to fetch me, saying, "I knew she was on the wrong bus when all the other little blond ones got off, and she was still there."

Two years later, Brian and I were bussed to the newly built school with an almost all white student body. Most were daily skiers with season passes their parents paid for. Brian and I had passes because our parents worked there. We were aware of the difference and felt superior.

President Ford's helicopter landed while we looked on from Vail Mountain through the trees. Our parents were Republicans – our father said no one gave him anything, so no one else should need welfare either, and our mother said people didn't have enough faith to carry them through difficulties.

As our mother's children, Brian and I saw God everywhere. In the sky of a rainy day in the mesas of Grand Junction, God seemed to drag his giant paintbrush from the deep slate sky to the mountains. We saw the cross in all things: the snow-filled crags of rocky mountains, windowpanes, telephone poles, barbed wire fence posts, livestock gates, the stuff of our childhoods.

God rained down punishment and reward. All things could be traced to wrath.

When our father said he didn't believe in God, we cried and were afraid for him. We wanted him to believe in God the way we wanted him to stop smoking. Both were deadly, but our father didn't like people telling him what to do, even out of love.

He'd been raised by a hard-hearted father. He said we should be grateful, and we were to know we'd never be as tough as he was.

Our father said things to induce guilt.

"I paid for my own dental work." When we went to the dentist.

"Had a paper route so I could buy food." When we sat down to dinner.

"My dad hit me so hard I saw stars. No, he hit me so hard I saw stars on my stars." To threaten us when we disobeyed.

"I took those beatings, and I turned out just fine. It's character building." To be even more threatening when we misbehaved again.

"You kids are spoiled rotten." When we got anything at all.

And he said we were thieves. "Who stole my hammer?" when he'd lost something.

As a child, paying for his dentistry, he barely had enough

money to build his homemade telescope. He attached a camera to it and took the first picture of Sputnik from American soil.

"I'll get you the article printed in the *Smithsonian*," he said while sucking in his cheeks, embers in his pipe burning, smoke seeping into the air and vanishing with our silent response, the way we navigated his contradictions.

Our father, like so many fathers, drank beer and watched football on Sundays.

One Sunday, I changed the channel because he fell asleep with a beer balanced on his belly.

"Turn that back," he yelled.

"You're not watching. You're sleeping," I said. Chin up defiant.

"You come here," he said.

"Why?"

"You're getting a spanking."

"No."

"Come here."

"No."

I ran. He didn't follow. I heard the game come back on. I hid behind the barn and watched the river that I once saw running red with heavy metals from upstream mining. I wondered how long I could stay hidden and how I would deal with my hunger. I didn't want to cry, but I did.

I was seven when he took out a loan for the all-time best construction business ever that didn't work out.

"God damn banks," he said, then had to sell the house.

Brian and I marked it as the saddest day of our young lives until other sad days replaced it. We left sadness there in the air, in the tractor trees, in the fields of thistle and alpine wildflowers, stone and memory.

We moved into a trailer park down the river in Edwards – the old highway on one side of the river with the post office and the trailer park, opposite I-70 and the gas station.

The goats went to live with the Motts on their land in Avon in the empty river bottom, hardly a town – with just them, the Vacation Bible School, and a store, open sometimes. The Eagle River had a chance to meander in the valley back then when it was green and void of hotels and malls.

The chickens were beheaded and frozen.

Mom said, "It all might be temporary."

Crackers, the only animal to make it out of the farm with us, had more kittens.

Mom said, "Watch how she teaches them to hunt. She keeps the mouse close, gives them practice killing, too."

After we'd moved into the doublewide, the kittens played under a big stuffed chair. Brian wanted to play with them, so he took a running jump onto the chair, smashing one kitten – broken bones, blood coming out of its mouth.

Our father took it outside.

"What happened," I said when I heard the yelling, the door slamming, Brian crying in his room.

"Dad's killing the kitten," he said through the door.

"Why?"

"I jumped on the chair and smashed it – it's all broken up!"

I said, "Where is it now?"

Brian sobbed. "Still alive outside – suffering. Dad spanked me."

I ran outside and as Dad walked out from behind the shed, he yelled, "Get back in the house," and moved to hide the kitten dripping blood behind his back, a knife in the other, unhidden, hand.

I ran back into the trailer. "Mom! Dad's killing a kitten."

"It's going to die anyway, honey," she said.

"You can't save it?"

"I can't."

Mom had saved things before. She'd killed things, too. She knew when to hold on to hope and when to move things along.

I told her Dad spanked Brian even though he didn't have to.

She looked at me. "How do you know this?"

"Brian told me."

She looked up from washing the dishes and said, "I told that man I'd take care of the killing and the boy, but he said he'd do it all. I told him not to spank that kid." She said it into the air, rather than to me.

And then I said, "Dad spanks Brian all the time for everything."

She had that look she had when she would say, "I have had just about enough."

She mostly stopped talking to Dad about then – just limited words for necessary tasks.

"Please, pass the pepper."

That sort of thing.

And she began to whisper and hiss. When she did the dishes, mostly – inaudible muttering and hissing arguments under her breath, shoulders hunched, dishes shined, dried, and put away. Quiet whispers. Furious hissing. I'd say, "You mad at me?" She'd say, "Why do you always think I'm mad at you?" More whispers. More hisses.

2. Strange Land

THAT SUMMER, MOM TOOK BRIAN AND ME OUT INTO Colorado. "Looking for a place to live," Mom said. We left Edwards, the cat in a crate. Crackers (we called her Fuffy) roamed the '71 Dodge van when we weren't driving. We wandered Colorado. We camped by the road, by rivers, under trees on private land, in campgrounds and RV parks.

Where is Dad, we asked, but she said, "He'll come soon, I think," and we didn't ask again, used to avoiding his anger and used to adventures without him. We began to live without him, and our mother didn't mention him for months. Brian and I spoke of him, but only to each other, in bits and pieces when we felt the loss and anger and confusion. "Where do you think he is?" and "Don't know" and "What's going to happen?"

"Watch the cat," Mom said, every time we got out to go to the porta-potties.

Fuffy sat on the dashboard watching bats and birds and guarding us against the night. Mom said, "She was a bobcat in another life."

Brian wrote ATTACK CAT on a piece of paper. People smiled at the tiny cat and the menacing words when they left their RVs and campsites.

Mom signed on with an archaeological dig in the ranchlands west of Cortez, filled with ancient dwellings of the people who lived there, the ancestors of the Pueblo people who encountered

Spanish conquistadors and lumberjacks and uranium mines. The archaeologists called the ancient people the *Anasazi*.

We parked under a small stand of trees in a wide red clay field. Millet, beans, and vegetable farmers cleared fields, leaving islands of stone mounds that meant an ancient dwelling lay buried there in the top layer of geological time and debris covering the floor of an ocean long drained away when the shore rose to become the Colorado Plateau.

The adults shoveled piles of red dirt out of the kivas, the round ceremonial structures, and up over the walls into giant piles that would be sifted through screens Brian and I were allowed to look through for small artifacts – bone, pottery, and stone. We imagined the people making these things, living whole lives, and dying, leaving that old world in the dust.

Professors gave talks at the dig, showing the skulls and bones filled with signs of disease and violence, telling us that life had been hard and often short. We sat by the ruins wondering about the voices they once contained.

A professor with weathered skin and deep wrinkles said only the men were allowed in kivas. We wanted to know why and how they knew.

"What about the little boys?" said Brian. "Could they go in?"

"What about the mamas with little boys?" I said. "Or their sisters?"

Mom and the professor talked and I listened, not understanding everything – I'd started reading Mom's archaeology books and collected *National Geographic*, imagining myself in the photos asking questions I couldn't find answers to in the long paragraphs. I memorized the figures and charts, the eras of time, the scientific names.

The archaeologists with their sun-dried skin, wide hats, and khaki clothes said, "The modern Indians are not the same Indians their ancestors once were."

"What's that mean?" Brian said.

"They mean the modern tribes have problems that ancient

tribes didn't," Mom said. "White people caused problems," and she told us some of the problems, but the problem that caught our imagination was alcoholism.

"Who brought the alcohol?" Brian said.

"The white man," she said.

"Which one? And why does anyone drink it anyway? Tastes terrible," which took the conversation in a whole different direction. Dad let us sip his Coors so we'd learn not to drink it.

"Sounds like your father's logic," she hissed.

The scientists and college kids were all white like us and from places far away. They lived an insulated life on the dig site and in their books and their methodologies and theories and didn't see the people who lived there – not the ranchers nor the pinto bean farmers, and not the Ute tribes, Navajo tribes, and other Native Americans. The scientists and college kids would leave this place and write about it when they got back to their other lives seeing it all as history – ten years later, a thousand years later.

But Brian and I didn't always stay to listen to their talking – we had rocks to climb and trails that needed to be walked, our eyes to the ground looking for arrowheads.

Sometimes arguments arose: the role of women, the uses of kivas, the patriarchy and the matriarchy, and the violence in man versus our better angels. Did people live here or only worship? How many generations? It all got heated sometimes. Raised voices. Hurt feelings.

"Male chauvinist pigs," Mom said under her breath so Brian couldn't hear, careful to tend his feelings.

Mom said, just to me, "If you're in charge of the food source, you are in charge," because the women in this ancient culture were in charge of 80 percent of the food source.

We imagined the ghosts of this place with stories we hadn't been told. We told stories and argued they were true – the way archaeologists did.

We lived in that world for part of a summer, gathering ghost stories, listening to scientists talk about ancient Indians while

American Indians from the Ute and Navajo and other tribes lived on nearby reservations or in neighboring towns and didn't work on the dig. Too young to understand the politics of academia or the horrors of genocide, I envisioned a hole in history – a time then, a gap, a time now. I couldn't imagine what filled it.

When the dig ended and school started, Mom began searching for a new job.

"What about our friends? What about school?" We cried. We howled. We fell silent. We adjusted.

We didn't return to Dad and the doublewide in the trailer park in Edwards. Instead we camped in our van in an RV park, by a Laundromat, across from the park in Cortez while Mom tried to find a place for us to live that didn't include our father. Mom dressed up in her big hat and round sunglasses, her loose skirt and sandals, walked Brian and me to the park where we'd wait while she tried to find a job, unless the drunk men were fighting or the police were there arresting them – the violence we feared and didn't want to see.

Mom said, "Don't talk to strangers," and she said, "Be polite." We had to navigate that conflict.

Staying away from the overly friendly men and the drunk men and the cowboys with their big trucks and hats, we watched for the unpredictable. We hadn't known enough cowboys and were still working out who we should fear.

We played on the swings, the merry-go-round, the teeter-totters, and played chase with the kids at the park with their moms nearby. Kids who could say shit (*chaa'*) and bullshit (*dóola bichąą'*) in Navajo and not just in Spanish, gave us words for our forbidden vocabulary.

Brian climbed trees with the boys, and I sat in the shade weaving dandelions, grass, and leaves into jewelry that never quite worked out.

Still jobless, Mom joined us when she came home from her search, she sat smiling in the sun, knees bent, her hands wrapped around them, watching us.

Cortez was a big small town – about seven thousand then, but the biggest town in the southwest until you got to Durango forty-five miles or so to the east, before the suburbanization of Durango and the long stretches of golf courses, condos, and concrete growing there now. The houses were grouped together in the middle of an expanse that stretches along Mesa Verde a few miles from the Sleeping Ute Mountain, guardian of the Ute Mountain Reservation.

At the grocery store, a checker and Mom were talking when the checker leaned in and said, "You let them play at the park alone? You know that's not a safe park."

Mom said, "Sure. They're fine."

"There are a lot of drunk Indians there," the checker said.

Mom scowled at the phrase "drunk Indians."

Once, Mom and I picked up her interview outfit from the dry cleaners across from the movie theater in Cortez. A man walked over and stood in line behind us. I could smell the alcohol. His neck bent from old age and maybe something else, he had to strain to look into Mom's eyes.

He said, "Hey lady, can I have a dollar?"

Mom pursed her lips, offering a stern sort of smile. I could see she wanted to be polite, but she couldn't give him money.

"I'm sorry," she said. The man turned to the next person in line.

The owner came from behind the counter and lunged at the old man. He was the kind of white man who didn't feel bad about American Indians or nearby reservations moved south to create borders for small Colorado towns or about anybody's poverty or drunken sickness. He was the kind of man like my father who used words Mom didn't allow Brian and me to say. The owner grabbed the man and threw him out the door and down the narrow doorway steps. Our father would've done the same thing, had done the same thing to people who "didn't belong on the job site" or on the mountain. The Vail Ski Patrol behaved like police on the hill and decided who belonged and who didn't.

Mom and I headed to the van.

"Can we call the police?" I said. His scraped skin bled through tears in his jeans, and his forehead gushed blood I could smell.

Mom said, "They'd only punish him."

"But, he's an old man." I remember hurried steps, getting into the heat of the van, red dust, plastic covering freshly cleaned clothes on a hanger.

The man limped to the corner, sat down on the curb, bleeding.

"Can't we help?" I said, but I knew the answer.

Mom didn't know what to do any more than I did. We drove away because we could. I watched the man as Mom backed away. I wondered about his family. His children. Glad my father wasn't there to be cruel, I still didn't feel right. Mom and I hadn't done any better. We left him still bloodied and alone. Looking back, I understand she wanted me to learn caution, but I've learned compassion and caution can, and must, coexist. When I become a ghost, I will forever sit with him, listening to his tears, bandaging his wounds if he'll allow it, if he can tolerate my presence. Maybe he'll go with me to taunt the dry cleaner man who surely resides somewhere bone-melting hot.

Hail pelted the roof of the van, thunder roared above us, lightning as tall as the mesas stretched to the high desert floor from God's angry clouds. Sun pushed through in places and rainbows threatened to brighten the vast sky and bring on heat.

We sped toward the vanishing point where we stayed in the RV park, safe from the dark under the neon sign.

When lightning and thunder rocked the van and Fuffy hid in the box inside the crate, I read the Little House books. Mom wanted me to be stronger, less sensitive, to learn some pioneer emotional toughness, and so she withheld compliments. Pa and Ma Ingalls didn't give out compliments to their children.

Mom said, "You can spoil a child with too many compliments. They come to expect it. They forget to be good for the sake of it."

Mom and I read those books together.

In the books, when Ma said what she said about American Indians, and Pa said what he said about American Indians, Mom said, "That's the way it was. Things have changed." I thought about the man at the dry cleaners, bleeding, and how things hadn't changed.

Brian went to church camp, up north again, where we'd just come from – a camp on the banks of the Colorado River near the confluence with the Eagle River. Our grandfather, Mom's dad, said Brian needed to go and ride horses and camp out so he could learn about nature and God and could hang around with children from "good families." Our grandfather said this in disgust, whether about our father's being gone or our not having a permanent home at the time, I couldn't be sure

Brian said, "It's okay if you don't write letters to me, Mom, because there won't be an address to send you letters at."

Mom told him not to end his sentences with prepositions and said, "I'll send you letters even if you can't answer them."

One night, I'd been sleeping when Mom was driving the van and it bottomed out and woke me up. I had been dreaming like I hadn't done since we began living in the RV park, the dusty sandstone place with the winding roads and the cowboys.

I wrestled my sleeping bag off and stumbled to the front. A deer bounded away from us in the headlights and veered off into the darkness. I smelled the sage and sandstone as the van groaned along.

"Where we going?" I said.

Mom said, "Gary's."

I saw a coyote, sitting at the edge of the high beams and thought about Gary.

"Why are we going to see him?" I said.

She said, "Because he's my friend," and she looked at me with her *don't start* look. I'd seen it many times because I was the kind of kid who talked. I could talk for hours without needing anyone to listen, but I hoped they would.

I talked to drown out the sound of the whooshing in my ear – my heart beat. I'd had it since I could remember. A swishing sound in my ear in time with my heart rate, inescapable and relentless noise that made my fear of the dark grow. There were times when I didn't hear the whooshing, when I experienced a precious silence.

I told Mom about it. She said, "You have water in your ear – that's all."

Gary was a real cowboy. Dad had been the opposite, a ski bum.

She had met Gary in the line at the grocery store.

We drove for a while until there were piñon and juniper outlines next to the road blocking out the stars on the horizon.

Gary stood in silhouette in the lonely bright ranch light, the light that every rancher had, usually by the barn, his truck parked beneath it.

"You'll be in the bunk house," he said to me.

"Oh, that'll be fun, sweetie. You'll have a whole house to yourself with Brian away at camp." Mom smiled in that direct way that ordered me to fight my fear of vampires and see this as a good thing.

But I failed to fight it. I said, "I don't want to stay there. Please, Mom. It's haunted."

They laughed. "Oh, he only said that to scare you last time."

Gary, not a tall man, opened the low hung door of the bunkhouse, barely above his head. We walked into the darkness. Gary lifted the lantern, and Mom carried the sleeping bag to the middle of the room and turned to me. The lantern created shadows I didn't care to see.

"Pick a bunk," Gary said.

Horns and antlers hung on the wall with a rifle above the door, the traditional fashion. "In case of Indians," Gary said with a smile and a wink, after he followed my eyes.

I couldn't see anything in the darkness when Gary and Mom left with the lantern, after he said, "Let's go, pretty-blue-eyed lady."

Mom kissed me goodnight, smelling like her rose night cream. Her hands were rough, strong and cold, and I loved them. I felt her hand print on my cheek and in my hair, shielding me from darkness. Unafraid of Indians, I wrapped blankets around my neck so vampires couldn't get to it and cried myself to sleep.

"Why did we have to go to Gary's last night?" I said when we drove away the next morning.

Mom said, "I already told you that."

"In the middle of the night?" I said. A repetition.

"Yes."

"Why?" I said.

"Never mind," she started her hissing then, shaking her head as she drove.

"I was sleeping really well when you woke me up last night and having a really nice dream about…"

"Would you stop whining about it?" she said.

"I was really tired." I looked out and counted the piles of stone, the crumbling ruins of ancient homes, wondering about long-dead children sleeping in stone rooms.

She said, "I mean it – you better stop this. Right now!" I stopped. She had that don't-talk-to-me-now mama look.

When Brian returned, we looked for a place to live, roaming through homes for sale throughout the southwest corner of Colorado outside the city limits of Dove Creek, Lewis, Dolores, Pleasant View, Yellow Jacket, and Cortez. Mom wanted us to be small-town kids.

"Sure is dry here," we said. We found fault with the sandstone and missed the rivers and streams and the rosehips and aspen.

But Mom, ever seeking bright sides, said, "You should have the chance to be big fish in a little pond."

We looked at a house with bullet-holed windows alone in

the middle of dry grass and wind, with water from a well and no plumbing indoors, and even Mom hesitated to live that kind of life.

One house, surrounded by acres of tall, dry grass that stuck in our socks, filled with emptiness and mannequins intrigued us all. Brian grabbed their hands to see if they would come off. Some were missing hands. They were all headless and naked.

Brian and I said, "Why are there mannequins?" over and over, but Mom didn't answer. She had things on her mind and mumbled them. We never got an answer, so we made up stories because that's what we did, Brian and I. Mom said we could clean it up and throw out the mannequins.

"Where will we take them?" we said, but she didn't know.

The house had running water but cost too much.

We settled into a rented house for the winter in Mancos, a town with a school and seven churches for the Catholics, Baptists, Methodists, Seventh-day Adventists, Episcopalians, First Christians, and Latter Day Saints. The railroad had left that small town like it had left many western towns when the mines were closed and the old trees were cut down, for the most part. It was temporary, we thought.

Mancos covered about half a square mile with the highway to the north and ranch lands and the Ute Mountain Indian Reservation to the south, slot canyons and the La Plata Mountains to the east and Mesa Verde National Monument to the southwest. West of that, the Colorado Plateau continued to stretch into mesas and high desert and more mountain ranges.

The town's name, Mancos, meant crippled in Spanish – a pejorative. We didn't take it as an omen, though we were a family that called out omens when we saw them.

Our father came to our new home – a rented house, then he left again, but he'd been gone three days before we asked about him.

"I guess I made the right decision then," she said.

They never said the word divorce in front of us, the same way they never fought so we could hear.

The house, facing south, did turn out to be temporary – the landlord didn't like renting to a divorced woman with children.

So, we moved to the other side of the block, facing north, into a rented singlewide trailer at the edge of an acre field with a long dirt driveway carved out by use – tire tracks guarded by small sentinel trees on either side The valley floor was a hundred-year flood plain. The construction and destruction of civilizations had gone on there since the tenth century. Trees were drowned, and trees were planted. Those trees at the end of the driveway seemed mighty for having survived the construction of the highway. The lot took up the northwest corner of the block. A long dirt alley split the block in half. The trailer ran parallel to it, a few feet off.

On the next block to the south was our church, and on the next block over from that was the school. In time, Mom would till a space for the garden along the barbed wire fence that split the acre in two but only ran part way across, as if the fence builders changed their minds mid-task. We had a barn where one of Mom's future boyfriends would attach a basketball hoop on the alley side. There were a burn barrel, piles of wood, and a small collection of appliances and bedsprings.

We walked east down the alley to go to school and west to go to church.

Saint Paul's Church reminded our mother of her childhood church – same creed, same saint – St. Paul was the reformed one, penitent. We felt the pity from others who considered us a broken family, and though they were loving, it stung of judgment. The Bible's edicts couldn't be rewritten. Mom played the organ. Music gave her a place to belong in the tiny white church with the red double doors, stained glass in some of the windows.

People at church helped us move into that trailer, putting Mom's bed by the big window at the front end of the trailer. Not as fancy a trailer as the doublewide in Edwards had been, but fancy wasn't the purpose of this singlewide trailer in Mancos. It was a temporary shelter for my mama, the roamer, for Brian, the dreaming-of-wilderness boy, and for me, the one who liked carpets and walls to stop the wind.

Pioneer ghosts whispered to us how lucky we were to find a place to settle down. The spirits in all those high mountain graveyards – filled with mamas and babies and soldiers. They whispered, "You're lucky to be alive. We had it so rough. We settled all of this for your sake. We died for you."

Our father visited one day on his motorcycle in the muddy, blossom-filled spring and drove Brian and me to Pikes Peak. Brian sat on the gas tank between his arms, and I sat behind, gripping the handles of the backrest.

He said, "You kids are lucky. My father never did anything like this with me."

Then he left and moved to California.

Luck and privilege are tricky things.

Mom fetched the piano from someone who'd stored it now that we'd settled. Mom kept a skull on the piano for a while. The piano had belonged to her mother. A man who liked our mother found the skull at a dig site and gave it to her to win her over. The man said the skull had belonged to a woman and based his opinion on the smaller size of the skull and the less pronounced ridge of the temporal line. We tried to name the skull, but nothing stuck.

We'd ask her, "What was your name?" but she kept it to herself. I played Pachelbel's *Canon in D* and imagined her life in sad, beautiful vignettes. I wondered how far she'd come from her homeland and where her mother lay buried, aware of the loneliness she must feel on top of a cold piano against the trailer wall.

BEFORE BRIAN AND I went to the cemetery to mark the spot where Mom's grave would be dug, I visited what had once been our two-acre farm. A plant nursery and a row of businesses now replaced the house, cottage, and barns, and the remainder of what had been pasture, but the surrounding mountains held meadows and forests, still bare of houses, protected for wilderness.

As I cried by the tree of my childhood, grieving, a man walked out to his car from the nursery and saw me and said, "You alright?"

"I used to live here before all this was here. The barn was there, the house over there. These two trees were Brian's and mine. We thought they belonged to us."

"The place has changed," he said.

"You from here?" I said.

"California," he said, and he saw the look in my eyes seeing his polo shirt tucked in to his leather jeans with a turquoise-laden buckle and cowboy boots – playing cowboy. "But, I've been here twenty years."

I nodded. Resigned.

So many new people claiming the place as theirs. So many more people in the world.

I wasn't from around there anymore, but I felt my western Colorado localness as if it were real. Even then. The belief in my own belonging had been a hard-won thing. I'd become part of the mesas and mountains, the sage and piñon, the alpine wildflowers and the rocks above timberline.

It was hard to let go of all that I had to let go.

Brian and I had been the inseparable children of a narrow wild river, chick spines, songbirds, firearms, and strong opinions.

I still resist letting go, believing in my belonging the way I used to believe in God.

But, it is all becoming ghosts.

Where do we bury our mothers when there is nowhere we belong? How do we settle with ghosts?

3.   Daughters and Sons

"YOU THINK YOU KNOW EVERYTHING," SAID BOBBY, THE bully.

"Do not," I said, children circled around me by the puddle-filled basketball court, chain nets clanging in the wind.

"You do," said Ryan, the smelly kid with thick glasses. We competed in class, first to raise our hands or first to be right.

"She does," said Ryan's friend, raising his chin at the beginning of each word.

"Yep," the popular girl, Melody, snapped her illegal bubble gum.

"Well," I mumbled, "Why wouldn't you want to know everything?"

"See?" said Melody, and they all laughed.

"Yep," said Matthew, the cute boy following Melody.

My polyester pants stuck to my socks, my hair crackled static, sweat pooled and dripped.

I said I was related to Nelson Rockefeller. Our last name was Nelson, so I connected some dots.

In fourth grade, I'd been the second most popular girl because my pretty best friend, Cindy, was most popular. I was nothing without Cindy.

Brian spent time alone in Mancos setting traps, climbing trees. The Mormon fathers took him into their world of badges and pinewood derbies so he became friends with their sons. I had a harder time of it. My know-it-all facade combined with a prepubescent body that expanded and contracted like the universe didn't help.

Before school started that fall, I walked across the gravel street to a house where I'd seen children and knocked on the door.

A woman with tight jeans, a western shirt with red piping, and sharp-pointed boots opened the door, and through a screen door with curved decorative metal that ended in sharp points said, "I'm Mrs. Rawlins." She had a thin smile, the forced kind.

"Mrs. Rawlins, do you have any kids I could play with?" I smelled coffee and butter and onions.

She didn't smile. Said, "Mm-hm. They're not here right now. You go home. I'll send my daughter over to play sometime."

But Rose and I played at her house. "My mom says we have to play here." Rose looked at her mom standing in the doorway to the kitchen, glaring. Thin and hard, tanned and tough-faced, she drank from her coffee mug and watched as we walked away into the living room.

We stood by the brick fireplace wall filled with pictures of short-haired boys and long-haired girls, cowboy hats and bolo ties, big belt buckles. Turquoise. Long-haired, blue-eyed Jesus with his thorny crown.

Leather belts and a fly swatter hung on the wall by a paddle, the words burned into it, "The rod and reproof give wisdom: but a child left to himself bringeth his mother shame. Proverbs 29:15."

From the kitchen, Mrs. Rawlins said, "I'm going out, Rose. Better keep outta trouble while I'm gone."

"Okay, Mom."

The door slammed shut, the truck turned over twice then started, the smell of exhaust filtered in, and Rose let out a small breath and softened and instead of her hard look like her mother's, for a second, I saw her sadness. But only for a second.

"This is where they hit us. You have to lie over the chair like this." She lay over the arms of the big stuffed chair and said, "We have to," in answer to my unspoken why.

Then she said, "Where did you live before?"

When I told her Edwards, close to Vail, she said, "Yeah, that's a different kind of place. Hippies and rich people and skiers."

"Not only."

She shrugged. "Mostly. Mom said your mom's not married. There's no divorce around here." I nodded the way you have to sometimes.

We moved closer to the wall with the belts, compelled, drawn in by the danger of it. "These are what they hit us with. They wet the fly swatter first."

"Why?"

"Because we're bad and kids should be hit or they grow up wrong. They hit us every day even if we don't do anything wrong, but they might only hit us once or softly. They say it's for all the things they don't catch us doing or for the things we're thinking about doing later. I'll do it to my children someday. We have to be better than other people."

I saw something in her eyes. A need to pull me in to this idea. Other people.

I stepped back, feeling sick and small. Mom spanked us, and it pushed me to anger, to scream into my pillow that I hated her, and to see her as a monster without mercy, but there was something more than the pain of punishment in the belts on these walls. Mom held mercy more often than not when it came to hitting us. These people held mercy as an exception.

"I think I'll go home now."

I left her standing in the middle of the room.

She got this little smile on her face, glad she scared me away. We would always have that kind of friendship.

I felt safer at the Whipples' house. They didn't have a belt wall. It smelled like Chihuahuas and the fourteen children born to Mr. and Mrs. Whipple.

Connie was my age, the second youngest in her family.

A line of family photos hung in the living room. Two frames contained names only, handwritten on tiny pieces of paper – babies who'd died.

A soldier, framed by chipped, gold-colored metal – the corners didn't join up, the photo old-timey.

We stood looking at photos, amid damp smells and piles of papers and clothes. Her father, his head in a newspaper. Her mother napped, Chihuahuas in her lap.

I whispered, "How old was he?"

"I don't know," Connie whispered.

"Which war did he die in?"

"My parents don't let us say how he died."

When I told Mom about the Whipples' house, she said no one could keep a tidy house with that many children and so, she said, "You better not judge."

I told her if she'd had a lot of children her house would still be tidy and she smiled.

Connie invited me over for chore night. Two hours and piles of dishes, meat fat stench, stuck spaghetti, clogging and unclogging the sink. It took me too many overnights to figure out to ask first about chore night.

I asked Mom, "Which war do you think he died in?" when I told her about the dead oldest brother.

Korea? Vietnam? She did the math and said, "If they don't want it discussed, then it shouldn't be discussed."

Mom asked if they were Mormon. I told her no way. She said, "Catholic?"

"No, they don't go anywhere on Sunday."

On Sundays, they camped in homemade tents under cottonwood trees, made hot chocolate and sugared coffee by the potful, sat in lawn chairs, and played with hula hoops. They laughed at everything and picked on me because I cried a lot.

"We're helping you," they said. "You're weak because you only have one brother."

Reading through the obituaries later, I found that the eldest died in a car accident. Mom told me of the importance of reading obituaries, a habit passed down from her father to her – an old businessman's trick, "You never know what you'll find out about a person from their deceased relatives," he said.

At night, Mom cried in the living room.

I went to her, nightgown billowing over the heat register, and reached out to hug her, but she said, "Go back to bed. I'm so tired."

"If you're tired, you should go to bed," I told her.

She said, "You! To bed!" Her eyes were wide in the half-darkness, her voice a raised hiss. She moved closer and I could feel her anger and power as she pointed me to my room. "I have to work in the morning. I have to work every day without sleeping enough. You go to bed. Now."

Swallowing the burrs in my raw throat, I went.

I dreamed that the three of us wandered, my brother and me following our mother's nightgown flowing in the wind across a soundless, airless desert.

On the way to her teaching job in Dolores, Mom found Hootie, a great horned owl, in the road and brought him home to nurse him back to health. He'd been hit by a car and had a teardrop shaped pupil in one eye. He perched on Mom's bedroom door, newspaper below, his head tilted. He fell softly to the floor without gliding. He walked on the ground like an arthritic man. He ran into walls.

Mom said the cats were safe from him. "He's not a hunter anymore," she said.

When the landlord found out, Mom drove Hootie to the Fort Lewis College biology lab in Durango.

"We can't lose this place, too," Mom said.

"What'll they do with him?" I said.

"You don't want to know."

I cried into my giant pile of stuffed animals.

I spent my after-school hours eating saltines and butter until Mom couldn't buy those anymore.

"You can't just eat all of these in one sitting," she said. "Go out and make friends."

"Nobody likes me," I said. "I say all the wrong things."

"You have to try harder," she said. "You have to count to ten before you speak."

Brian played in the alley that split the block in half, lined with fences, out buildings, a few trees, and a lilac bush. He played in the field of tall grass and in the one barely big-enough tree at the end of the long driveway. Sometimes I did cartwheels and handstands in the trailer. I pretended to always be on the balance beam in the Olympics.

That first Christmas, the priest stayed and delivered the midnight service in Mancos. He traveled between Cortez and Mancos, St. Barnabas to St. Paul, the prophet to the penitent.

We sat close to the aisle at the end of the pew in the back row.

I fidgeted, sure of a Christmas miracle – our father's return.

Mom had said, "Maybe. You just never know," when we asked.

I slid closer to her in the pew and said, "Can I go check?"

"Okay," I stood to step over her feet, careful not to trip on the prayer bench.

Strict with us in church, she sought to prove she didn't need our father to make us behave, seeing our good behavior as proof of her maternal skills and as a barrier to outside criticism for being a single mother. I should've known something was wrong when she let me walk up and down the aisle during church.

I slipped through the creaking inner doors, pushed open a red outer door and walked into the cold and dark, so many stars behind the great pine and the cloud of breath I let go.

Aware of unseen patches of ice, I stood at the top of the red steps and listened for his motorcycle, bought with the savings he took when Mom told him to leave for the last time. I'd thought he was a memory, that I was past missing him, but Christmas made me think of him the way Christmas makes us think of how a family should look – a mother, a father, a baby, even if that baby was actually kin to God.

But no Christmas motorcycle appeared, so I sat beside Mom, head on her shoulder – tender leniency.

"He's not here?" the priest asked me after the service.

"How did you know?"

"Well, I heard that door open at least five times."

"Oh."

"It's okay, you know. You have a father in heaven who always loves you and is always with you."

Mom smiled through watery eyes, a couple of ranchers blew their noses and one tousled Brian's hair, and another put his hand on his small shoulder. Women held us in a circle of perfume and church dress clothing, scarves and coats, soft-gloved hands.

I watched Mom's breath hang in the cold air as we walked home. We crunched through the snow, across the ridges of tire tracks, Brian skidding along, running and jumping into small snow banks, anything he could find to gain even more altitude here at seven thousand feet above sea level.

"Dad's not coming, is he?" I said.

My eyes blurred in the cold, making the Milky Way go watery, smudged into one wide streak of light.

"I don't think he is."

Brian chased away a cat who'd come to us for a pet.

Mom handed us a Christmas card when we got home.

"He sent this to you kids. I didn't want to show it to you before," her voice soft.

The words in red curving print, "Across the Miles," a glittering mountain scene with a curving road disappearing into it. She'd known, she told us, but hadn't had the heart to face us.

Mom held us while we sat in the dark watching the blinking lights on the Christmas tree.

She said, "We will keep our traditions."

4. A Familiar Kind of Forgiveness

THE GEOGRAPHY GAVE US NEW TRADITIONS. EVERY CHRIST-mas Eve day, we walked out into a forest with our tree permit.

We took the saw. Mom wore her leather gloves. Mom found one she liked. "How 'bout this one?"

Brian didn't like it. Said, "Nah, too bare on this side."

"We always have a bare side," I said.

They both looked at me with surprise and annoyance. "We face the bare side to the wall anyway," I said.

"You have to be positive," Mom said, because this might be the year that we find a perfectly symmetrical, conical tree.

Brian said, "You're a negative Nellie."

"No. I'm just saying there are bare sides on all these trees and the bare side always goes to the wall. It's no big deal if it's not perfect."

Mom looked at me. Angry. I looked away, ashamed.

"You can just go sit in the car if you're not having fun, but we're staying out here," Mom said.

I fought tears. Dumb thing to cry over – being misunderstood. I wasn't being negative. Bare sides on trees are real things.

I was having fun. Now, I felt ashamed and I failed to find the right words among the too many words I said.

I stomped along silent behind them. It was quiet.

The tree sap and the needles smelled sweet. Pitch like caramel.

Mom got down on her knees and sawed the tree down. She

was strong. Only when my brother was older did she give up her place and let him cut it down.

But we were thankful for the snow, the time together, the saw, the sap.

My brother liked to drag the tree through the snow because he was the man and that was a man's job. He was the man in our family, wearing his jean jacket and flannel underneath, his snow boots.

The tree went into the back of the van, the door handles were roped together, a red paisley scarf was tied to the top of the tree all the way home on those gravel roads and then on the highway.

We put up the tree on Christmas Eve, never before.

At dinner, at the round kitchen table, the tiny metal angels flew in small circles, a soft dinging of bells as you'd think an angel would sound.

The angels hung from a disk mounted on a metal post some inches above another disk, their small planet. Their heaven moved by the fire of candlelight. Their world revolved when we lit it. They flew, blowing the horns that were attached to their golden lips.

One candle lit for each week of Advent. The first candle, the first week, moved them, but by the fourth week and the fourth candle, they would pick up speed, the dinging growing louder as we felt the heat of Jesus' impending arrival.

Then we went to church. There was incense and a familiar forgiveness. There were bent knees and there was a time for standing and passing the peace. All those hands that connected us to each other and to something more.

After church, we walked back to the trailer and sat on the floor by the tree.

Mom read *The Night Before Christmas*. Reading the story and turning the pages was all familiar. It was a dream we dreamed together. A story about people who live in a house we could only imagine. A story about people who love magic as much as we did. A story about a man who believes and is rewarded for his belief.

That's what we wanted. And what, in the reading of the story, we received.

We did this until our last Christmas together, until everything changed.

TWICE MOM TRIED to get child support through the legal system, but instead she got letters that deemed our father unable to pay.

"Unable to pay," she said over and over.

"Nobody ever asks me if I'm unable to pay. Oh, you're unable to pay for these groceries? Go ahead and take them anyway."

I remember one year during tax time, Mom said, "We're above the poverty line. I get to pay taxes!"

She wanted us to dance with her. She rattled the trailer with her Charleston, her Swim, her two-step, and her Hustle.

She told us our father wanted her to pay for us to visit him, but she couldn't. She would, she said, if she could.

We visited him when I finished seventh grade. He took us to the beach, oil-slicked, stinking of fish and trash. We'd thought it would be different. Dad's house had deep carpet, his roommate had a massive fish tank, he had a yard with a tall fence. Dad wrestled with us. He threw me on the ground so hard my head rang. Brian got hurt and cried and then got mad and pushed Dad to the ground, small and ferocious. Dad said, "Atta boy!" They laughed when I said I had a headache.

We sat in his big black truck – brand new.

Mom said Dad moved to California with the other dads to get out of child support payments.

Right then, though, in the truck parked by a suburban sidewalk, our dad wanted to talk – the first talk he'd ever had with us. As a talker, he talked at us, not to us.

"I wanted to keep the family together, but your mom wanted a divorce. When people get divorced, they have to decide who gets to keep the children."

I felt a new kind of panic. I didn't understand what was happening, what could happen.

We were in California, a place so filled with people and cars that we huddled together, my brother and me. I couldn't remember in that moment how to find my way back to the airport from there. As the older, the responsible one, I should've paid closer attention.

"I think you kids are old enough to decide who you live with."

I thought I'd cry, so I started talking to keep that from happening. In that, I was my father's daughter. I said, "We want to live with you." I didn't want to lose my father.

Dad said, "It's not really possible." I could hear train whistles, sirens, and car horns in that deep and complete rejection. My heart a sack of blood and tissues, sore and wounded, with Brian's skin like smoke beside me.

Dad looked straight ahead, out the front window, fingers woven and his hands resting on the steering wheel.

Silence.

"It's best for you to live with your mom."

I studied the four-count whoosh in my ear, distracting myself from the guilt of betraying Mom, relieved we'd go home to her. If Dad had wanted us, he could've kept us.

On the plane, Brian and I got extra peanuts because in those days we were still unique – children traveling between divorced parents. I popped the peanuts open and they flew into the aisle and into a lady's big hair and bounced off a man's hat. We laughed until I got nauseous, as usual. Brian said, "You always ruin everything with your fragile problems." But he laughed when people handed us their little white vomit bags. "The looks on their faces, Jenny. You should see. It's like they're scared of you," he kept laughing. I used up a lot of those bags.

Mom picked us up in Durango and we saw elk on the way home. We stopped and listened to the long eerie whistle of a bull elk, his breath floating into the sky. Gunfire echoed in the distance. All that geography.

We had to find ways to belong to that town, the few, the prideful, the related, as Brian said. In a town of eight hundred people friendship was scarce. Employment opportunities few and far between.

Born a Midwesterner, Mom cooked her way into the Mancos Valley community: Chocolate no-bakes, strawberry jello with cream cheese layers, pies, casseroles, cookies. She added the foods of southwest Colorado – enchiladas, chili, sopapillas.

"When do we get to have one?" we said when she cooked.

"After everyone else gets one," she said. I whined. She said, "Don't be selfish."

One day, Mom said, "Mr. Culp made me witness while he disciplined a child today."

"Did you stop it?"

"Oh, Jenny. I didn't have a choice. You don't understand because you don't have to pay the rent or buy food."

She walked out to the garden to pitch rocks over the fence. Most of our gardening meant pitching rocks, clearing out some space for corn and for strawberries. Some sweetness.

Mom came home late one night after school.

She said, "Some things have happened at school. Some people wanted a union and they were fired right then and there at the board meeting."

"Did you get fired?"

"I didn't."

"Why?"

"I don't want to talk about it, honey. It's complicated."

Silence.

She said, "I just want you to know that the people who got fired aren't bad people, no matter what you hear about them."

That first autumn, we watched the La Plata Mountains turn orange and red in waves.

Mr. Culp, the sixth-grade teacher and school principal, carried a wooden paddle, his "swat board," he called it, and slapped it against his hand.

We were prey to his predator. He'd smile, standing beside the teacher at the front of the room. His eyes were kind and his smile friendly while he slap, slap, slapped. Terrifying.

He had a fear and hatred of Russians, the way television newscasters did, the way authors of *Time* magazine did, the way newspaper journalists did, but the journalists and newscasters and Russians were far away. We felt Mr. Culp's angry heat on our necks when he breathed our names into them, heads bent over pencil and paper – all that fear hidden beneath our chicken-bump skin.

Timmy, Kevin, Brent, Rodney, and Billy got swats weekly. The boys from the poorest of the poor families. None of them belonged to the temple or to any church. I don't remember them being all that misbehaved.

Bobby Denton got swats every day. He grew up in red house by a field of trucks and heaped cars by the road running north to Dolores.

"My dad hits me harder," he told us at recess.

The boys went to the office for the swats. In the fall and spring, we heard the whack through the open windows.

I stayed away from Bobby, the bully. Big. A spitter.

"I'll make you boys into good men," Mr. Culp said. Slap of the wood to his hand. I knew it had to sting.

He didn't let us speak a word without permission. Speaking out of turn meant a swat. Asking most kinds of questions meant a swat. Girls got swats, mostly, for this, but once five girls got swats for sledding on the hill at recess in dresses.

"Is everyone being good today?" He said when he looked into each room when he became principal only and didn't have to teach anymore.

"Oh, yes. Everyone," the teacher would say.

Brian and I hadn't known any principal like that before.

We talked about him while we burned the trash in the barrel by the barn, a new chore for us.

When we lived near the Vail Valley, it was the seventies and education meant mini-classes – cooking, origami, macramé, skiing, and field trips to wildflower meadows. It was all colors and narrative reports, satisfactory and outstanding and at worst an N for Needs Improvement. That newly built school we were bussed to was progressive, preparing students for possibilities. We'd put on a school production of *Free to Be ... You and Me*.

In Mancos, the seventies arrived later. Teachers gave letter grades. Children learned through textbooks, rote memorization, and discipline with strict rules, straight lines, the Pledge of Allegiance, moral certainty, no discussions, no show and tell. We went on one field trip in sixth grade to Mesa Verde National Monument, seven miles away. Two of the kids had never left Mancos before. The school prided itself on discipline, preparing students for jobs.

Mancos was heads turning when you walked in the door of the P&D convenience store or the post office or the café. Mancos was who'd parked in your driveway with out-of-state plates and what the bride and her mother wore at the wedding and who survived whom published in the weekly two-sheets of newspaper. Mancos was a river valley with ghosts of boom and bust, trails in, trails out. Mancos was moving the border of a whole American Indian reservation for white settlers and for their many churches for so few souls, for railroads, and for itself because it could.

Mancos was haven to Mormon fundamentalists and the Second Amendment in cross stitch and engravings and everyone in closets and no privacy and artists as painters of old western motifs and children of belt-smacking parents and violence as love. Mancos was knowing who's in town, who's leaving town, and who'll never come back. Mancos was wanting more and also wanting nothing to do with the outside world. Mancos was belonging to mythology through genetics or land. Teenagers and young adults shot handguns by the water tower on the hill where the track team ran repeats.

Mancos was tourists saying, "This is such a beautiful area," making Brian and me shake our heads, disappointed because we couldn't leave. They didn't understand the more beautiful place we'd lived.

The kids in Mancos didn't have goats or chickens or ski passes. They had cowboy boots and many siblings. They had religion and discipline. We started to change, too. More religion, more discipline, because it mattered more or maybe we just noticed it more or maybe something else happened.

When Mom hissed, I'd say, "Are you mad at me?"

"No," hiss, hiss, whisper.

"You sure?"

Whisper. Hiss. "Tell your brother to go burn the trash."

We took the trash out, walked down the two-tire-track driveway along the trailer, past the cat ladder, saying hi to whichever cat sat there waiting to hop into the tiny window near the roof of the trailer. Then we crossed the dry grass to the burn barrel. Brian lit the fire with Ohio matches, made right there in Mancos, Colorado. We watched things burn and listened to the whisper and hiss of the fire.

Mom and Brian got angry at the television, at the loud women there, women like senators and women's rights types.

"Women should never shout," Mom said.

Brian said, "I hate loud women. Why are they so angry all the time? Need husbands, I think. They're jealous of prettier women."

When my brother said that, though, Mom would hiss again. I wished she'd let him have it, but she never did. Mom and I had to navigate what we could yell about and when. Brian was freer to roam with his rage because "Boys will be boys" and "Whistling girls and crowing hens always come to some bad ends." When Brian was frustrated, he grabbed my hands, laced my fingers together and held his hands over mine and pressed until my knuckles felt like they'd pop. He did it to Mom, too. He sat with Fuffy sometimes, even through his teen years, biting her paws, and Mom couldn't stop him.

Mom and Brian dreamed they were ancient American Indians living not far from here.

"I was a woman holding a dying baby," Mom bragged.

Brian said, "I killed a deer with three arrows."

"You're never in the dream." Mom looked at me.

"Mine either," Brian said.

"Nope."

"Never."

There were times at the dinner table when Mom said, "Save that for your brother."

I wanted my mama to get food stamps. She wouldn't. "I'm a Republican."

"But Mom, it'd be so much easier. We wouldn't feel so sad about food."

"It's not right. None of us are starving. You could even lose some weight, you know."

"I know."

Sometimes she wanted ice cream, but dinner and dessert was too expensive, so she bought ice cream for dinner, an impossible thing to complain about.

It was a time of complicated cycles of poverty of the mind and of money – being broke, having enough, wanting only what we needed, preparing for the next cycle of being broke, but wanting more and needing more and having ideas and dreams just like everyone else – all of it, complicated. There were ranchers with multiple snowmobiles and trucks who said they really suffered when even one calf was taken by predators and there were people without stable housing who had big trucks. There were others who said they couldn't get to the dentist but they partied and drank and kept themselves up on cowboy boots and had a collection of firearms. Our mother had opinions about all of those decisions that other people made, but when we had opinions, she said not to judge.

She sang the song by Dolly Parton "A Coat of Many Colors." She wanted us to understand that there were many levels of poverty and suffering, and she wanted us to be grateful, especially at that time, when some things in our lives were harder than they had been.

Brian became the man of the house.

The guns went under his bed.

I spent a lot of my time worrying about everything that could be worried about.

I had wanted to be tougher like Mom and Brian and to be some kind of western Colorado small-town kid.

I was for a while.

II. Seeking Redemption: Becoming Mancos

5. Supine

"YOU DON'T BELONG HERE," PATTY SAID. "AND YOUR MOM'S a teacher." She spat the word onto the ground. In that town being a teacher meant living off the tax money paid in by the Smiths, Pickens, and Noland families, the oldest white settler families, who claimed pioneer family blood.

I lay on the snow-packed gravel street looking up at her. I struggled to stand. "Stay down," she said.

I stood from the frozen road covered with a fresh layer of snow. She pushed me down again. "Stay down, I said."

"I hate you," I cried, shaking – angry at myself for my weakness. My hat crooked, my nose running, my mitten lost. Patty laughed.

I stood and she pushed me down again. "Stay down," she said again and again, every time I stood.

She walked away when she got tired of me standing up. I didn't have pioneer blood, but I could act like it.

Connie watched the whole thing from the side on a snow bank, then came over to us to walk home with me – she and I were going that way when the trouble started. She said, "Well, you stood up to her," and Patty, overhearing her, cackled. I felt like granite and rage, but nothing could be done. "See ya, Patty," Connie yelled and put her arm around me. Connie always tried to stay on good terms with everyone, being the thirteenth of fourteen children.

Patty lived with her mom, who moved a few times the same

way that we had – out of necessity: landlords, too few and too small paychecks, seeking dreams.

Patty had had it out for me that day. She had it out for everyone most days. She picked different people at different times, unpredictably, like all terrifying things. It was my turn more often than others. I didn't like that she could do whatever she wanted. Powerful, pretty, popular, and a rancher's daughter, she had a hard-luck story. She had it all.

Her father, who had a new wife and let Patty live with them sometimes, between a Smith and a fourth-generation rancher, a descendent, an heir to so much land, owned his place, the piñon, the grazing land and the high blue sky, snow mobiles, big trucks, gun racks.

I wanted to belong to this place the way she did, the way she thought she had a right even though she was born in Las Vegas with its golf courses, huge hotels, casinos, and decorative water features in the desert. She moved to Mancos at the age of four. I was a Coloradoan, born six hours away by car, but the distance was more than just the land traveled across, the slick rocks, the red canyons, and the mountains to the east and the vast high desert to the west.

We'd never lived in a town as big as Mancos, with its eight hundred people. Before that, we'd lived outside of Minturn, a town of five hundred, and in Vail, a town of five hundred at the time, then we lived in Edwards, a town comprising a post office, a gas station, and the trailer park.

Patty was four years old and lived in Las Vegas when she swam in the pool with her little brother and her mother went inside the way people do just before disaster, "Just to answer the phone." Her baby brother drowned.

Patty said she couldn't remember anything about it.

Mom said, "It's just as well, but it really doesn't seem possible. Would be better that way, I suppose."

I said, "She's so mean. Why does she get to be so mean?"

Mom wanted me to see Patty's hard life through a good Christian lens and to understand something bigger.

I said, "My life has been no bed of roses." Mom laughed. She didn't understand. I wanted to fight Patty or to change her. I wanted her to stop being so cruel. I thought someone could make her change.

Patty had me believing that the best I'd be able to do would be to get up whenever she pushed me down.

When we moved to Mancos, Mom made less money, and the ski resorts were farther away, so we became hikers – these mountains were wilder and free.

We hiked to the top of Shark's Tooth Peak, leaving the van at the trailhead far to the side of the dirt road, where the gravel is loose, boulders at the trailhead.

Mom and Brian hiked ahead – fast. I trailed along among the pine and cedar trees. As we climbed, rocks were smaller and sharper and the trees diminished in size and number until we passed the line where they could no longer grow.

Mom and Brian stopped in the hot sun under a steel blue sky. I watched them cross a field of stones. Mom turned and waved to me, and I waved back. They'd catch me on their way down. I turned to face the valley, watching and remembering and documenting in my diary.

Another peak stood next to this one, shoulder to shoulder – people, mountains and mesas, and the desert on the edges of everything west. The wide sky stretched out over all of it, high and open. In this thin air, we breathed deep.

I sat on a boulder and observed the chirps and tweets of small animals and the scream of a hawk. I thought of skin walkers, the mythical-maybe-real-maybe shape-shifting lycanthropes the Ute and Navajo kids told us about on the playground. The most frightening thing about the skin walkers was their speed. I called them skin runners until a mean-laughing child corrected me. The raptors circled in a clear cold sky. I thought about the lives of muskrats and their kin. I listened to the wind and the silence of no wind, named a few clouds by their cartoon likeness, and then they were gone. I sang sometimes – soft. Pop songs, church songs, and Kenny Rogers's "The Gambler." I sang that a few times.

And I sat in silence. I know I had that goofy smile on my face that Brian made fun of when I watched TV.

Mom and Brian returned unafraid of skin walker predator bird shadows.

"You shoulda come up with us."

"You missed quite a view."

"Miles and miles of peaks and valleys."

"Stuff you can't see from here."

"Yeah. I liked it here, though. Plus, I couldn't keep up."

"Yes, you can. You just have to try harder," Brian said.

"Let's leave her alone, Bri. She's doing the best she can."

We hiked back down into the trees and back to the dusty van.

On the way home, down the dirt road in the La Plata Mountains, we sang Dolly Parton songs. Mom and I loved "Jolene" the most.

Our first winter in Mancos, I took my ice skates down to the river where I found small patches of ice between the rocks, safe from the rapids in the middle. I got good at spinning in small spaces, careful of the river rocks around me. I spun on those patches until the ice skates became so tight on my feet that I couldn't balance in them.

We couldn't afford to replace the skates – less money, fewer choices.

It wasn't a problem like the food and rent problem, but it hurt in a way I couldn't speak to for lack of clarity, and wouldn't for the shame of whining.

In the Vail Valley, we skied on Sundays. In Mancos, we went to church.

In church, we heard a perfect silence – thin, crisp pages turning, the suppressed coughs of people in a sacred place, a kind of reverence for everyone else's need for that silence. Everyone taking care of everyone in that way. The priest slurped the last of the wine and chewed the bits of Jesus' leftover body accompanied by the thud of books being put back in the bookrack behind the pew. I felt ashamed of my thoughts, words, and deeds, and by turns I also felt free.

Mrs. Weaver said, "I've never seen a child listen so well in church."

Mom nodded and smiled. "She does, doesn't she?"

I heard horror and beauty there and felt it. Church shattered me then held the shards.

Mom learned the piano as a child in Minnesota.

She played for the people of that small church, attendance of twenty-five souls on Christmas and Easter. She played every Sunday that she could make it to church.

She woke up early, walked out past the lilac bush, petted the neighbor's wiggling, yellow lab, to the next block over. With her church key to the heavy, red doors, she turned the heater on and walked back home until the little church warmed up enough for her to play the organ without having to wear gloves.

Mom said, "I really don't think that idle hands are the devil's workshop," but in life, she kept her hands moving – stitching, fixing, gardening, washing, cleaning. Macramé pot hangers and granny square blankets in the seventies, and in the eighties down vests and booties, stuffing it all with tiny white feathers and burning the edges of the fabric to keep them from unraveling.

She cried over money and we skimped on things. Sometimes we went skiing anyway, but then she'd cry about money at the end of the week. She wanted the life she'd come to Colorado to live. Sometimes she made it happen despite the lack. We borrowed. We waited things out. We ignored the phrases "How could you" and "Not supposed to" and "Well, I wish I could."

But, mostly, everything had changed. We lived closer to quieter things, hours from any freeway entrance.

She made a point of understanding the ghosts in the area: in Minnesota, her mother and the ghosts of Vikings that our father felt kin to; in Vail, the ghosts of skiers dead by avalanches, miners and trappers and wanderers; in Mancos, the ghosts of ancient and modern-day American Indians and the wives and children of the Mormon religious pioneers and soldiers.

Sometimes, when we were supposed to be asleep, Brian and I would talk late into the night. Sometimes he read stories he wrote – he wanted to be a writer. We missed the farm and the other part of Colorado with its higher peaks and deeper snow. We complained about Mom, wondered about Dad and God and our problems.

On those nights, Brian crawled down the hall, past the man buried in the wall right outside my door. I believed a man lay buried there in the paneled wall between hall and Brian's room – there was something about the doorway, farthest from the outer doors, and something about the stories we told each other about previous owners – maybe one of them died in the trailer. No one could tell us for sure. When I got to that doorway where the man was buried, I ran and jumped into my room to avoid his bony reach. The trailer hadn't moved for years. Mom said it wasn't a trailer, wasn't a mobile home because it couldn't be moved. She said it was un-nameable and immovable. I thought that sounded a lot like God. I was a child of superstition and faith.

I had my own room with a window to the alley and the backyard with a lilac tree and a swing set without swings, where I did chin-ups during my skinny times. Mom slept in the living room so I could have a room to myself, the master bedroom of our singlewide. She woke from nightmares sometimes. "Vampires," she said. "There were vampires on the ceiling and coming up through the floor."

Brian had his own room, too, where he played heavy metal.

As we'd always done, we spent hours together doing nothing, accustomed to having only each other for company.

At night, when Mom's light went off, Brian crawled to my room to talk, but maybe also to practice for the army, for the war he'd fight and win. He was crawling to someday save his life and the lives of the men around him. That was one of his dreams. We were children of just wars fought, of soldiers revered.

We belonged to the sandstone and snow created by change. The sands of ancient water bodies and high deserts settled and compacted by other minerals and colored by iron oxide. People traveled there to the sculpted sandstone to see it, to be changed by it, made more serene. We told stories about the place to find our place in it and grew possessive and protective, wary of too many tourists, too many hiking feet, too many souls seeking quiet salvation, adding noise with their footfalls.

Miles of power lines cut through the desert.

We were home where the mesas gave way to mountains. The sandstone sculptures, black against the night blue sky that gave way to the star-capped La Plata range.

Every summer, the garden grew more rocks. Brian and I were required to spend a half hour every Saturday in April and May pitching rocks over the fence into the dry, grassy field. A half hour felt like an entire morning to us. Brian wished to be wandering and maybe hunting or trapping small animals, and I wanted to be watching television, dreaming of romance and hoping myself thin, doing handstands against the trailer paneling.

Mom pitched rocks, wearing her wide-brimmed hat, a pair of octagonal sunglasses, cut-offs, and one of her homemade halter tops, her shoulders burned and peeling.

"I know you," Brian said to a rock he squeezed in his hand. He threw it and said, "And stay out!" It almost reached the highway. "Ornery rocks."

"Nice throw," Mom always said when Brian threw a rock a long way.

"Why are there so many rocks?" Brian said.

"God's wrath."

Brian said, "These are God's Easter eggs and these rocks have just been laid." He had a way of bringing rocks and eggs into conversations together as a segue to his egg joke – that I'd been born from an egg southwest of Mancos, between two rocks named

Elephant's Feet near Tonalea, Arizona, just off the side of the highway.

"The elephant laid the egg and when you broke out of it, she looked down and got so scared she jumped out of her feet."

"Mom!" I said, looking for comfort.

She said, "Yeah, I know, honey. But I'm out of it. You two work it out."

She said that to us as often as it needed to be said. "Work it out. You two have to figure things out for yourselves."

So we pitched rocks from our stony garden over the barbed wire fence watching the grasshoppers jumping and telling stories and working things out.

We became a different kind of country. A different kind of rural. Town rural. Not ranch rural. We loved the elk more than cattle, open space more than fences in parcels. When we saw a wild stream, Brian saw wild trout and freedom, and I saw cold, clear water to drink in cupped hands. When a rancher saw a stream, he saw a water source for cattle, for feed, for settling, for keeping from flooding into spaces the rancher owned. That's how we were a different kind of rural.

At school, there were three lunch ticket colors. Blue for the people who could afford full price, yellow for the reduced price, and red for the free lunch.

We almost always had yellow. I remember having red a few times. Not often.

"It's such a terrible experience – they ask these personal questions," Mama said about the free lunch tickets.

When I asked for lunch tickets, Mom cried and said, "Already?"

"Yeah." I felt ashamed of my needing and my hunger.

She didn't tell me that it wasn't my fault like I wanted her to.

We continued to adjust.

We lost things sometimes, even in the trailer we couldn't find them again.

"Poltergeists," Mom said, when things went missing. These ghosts followed our ancestors from old Europe.

"We should have turkey on Thanksgiving, ham at Christmas, lamb on Easter. That's the way it is with Christians," she said.

But we ate venison.

Mom sprinkled German words in her vocabulary from time to time.

She spoke Spanish to us often, but we answered in English.

She said "Pioneer women had to leave their pianos on the trail," and "in the Midwest, all the young girls I knew were thin." She'd nearly lost her piano in the move away from our father. She'd always been thin, always on a diet to lose weight. She used these phrases to shame, as weapons, as reminders of how good I had it and to tell me what kind of woman I should be.

But in other moments, she said, "People just didn't have enough information about child development." She said this when she told me her parents had tied her little hands to the bed so she wouldn't scratch her eczema, and also when she told me she wasn't allowed to say goodbye to her mother, who died of breast cancer when Mom was a teenager.

And then she'd revert again, saying, "Children should be seen and not heard. Kids used to work hard. Nowadays, kids have things too easy. I should make you kids do more chores."

She wanted us to have a cultural heritage, a mythology to cling to now that we had so few left in our family, and the farms full of hard work were gone. She was alone to carry on all those traditions.

Our American flag was displayed on many holidays. Mom unfolded the triangular red, white, and blue cloth. She set the metal pole in the bracket next to the door and attached the flag through the loops with the rope.

We sat on the steps, watched the dew dry, and felt the heat rise, smelled the sage and sandstone drifting to us over the vastness. And we listened to the flag flap gently in the breeze.

I spent the night with Patty on her birthday. Her mom was out all night and didn't come back until after I went home.

Mom said, "Patty's mom lets her boyfriends live in the house with Patty there."

Mom was so mad she couldn't speak. She sent me to my room so she could think.

I spent the time talking to the crucified Jesus on my wall – not about Patty's mom being out all night, but about the things we did while she was out.

"It wasn't my fault," I told him. Patty and I and some other kids had gone out and knocked on people's doors and then run.

When Mom came back to my room at the end of the trailer and said, "I talked to Patty's mother."

"What did you say?"

"Never mind. That's between us. You're not to go over there to stay the night. Everything you do in this town will be noticed. I have to work here. As a teacher, I'm supposed to be a good mom, a good citizen of this town. Beware your reputation because it affects mine."

Mom never let boyfriends stay in the house. I was to believe she never slept with her boyfriends. When Mom explained sex, she said, "The man sticks his penis in the woman's vagina," and when Brian and I pressed for more information, she said, "When they're married."

Patty's mom had mean boyfriends and bruises. The look in her eyes was a tough-woman, ever-unhappy look.

Patty stayed the night with her father sometimes when her mother ran off with a new boyfriend, but Patty's stepmother didn't like her.

Mom said, "We don't always get along – you and I – but I can't imagine ever putting you out of the house the way Patty's step-mother does."

When Patty and I were in a friendly phase, I told her Mom said I was fat, selfish, and talked too much.

Patty said that my mom was judgmental. "She thinks she's better than my mom."

I said, "Yeah, she's judgmental."

When Patty and I were enemies, she called me fat and selfish, and said I talked too much.

Patty and I had a complicated relationship.

6. Kneel

MR. ADCOCK, THE BUS DRIVER/SHOP TEACHER/DRIVER education/hunter safety instructor, passed out pages from hunter safety handbooks. He demonstrated the supine, kneeling and sitting positions for hunting, holding an imaginary rifle, cocking a phantom trigger, seeing deer. He threw blocks of wood at us when he got angry, when we made mistakes or asked questions we shouldn't have needed to ask because he'd already been over that, or if we disagreed or wanted to disagree because we had some point we thought could be correct, or at least worthy of a question. His throwing things wasn't unusual – the chemistry teacher threw erasers, and the social studies teacher dropped textbooks – BAM! For the same reasons. We weren't too old for corporal punishment, we were reminded, but like nuclear war, we pushed fear of it down.

Mr. Adcock told us hunting stories about heroes and idiots and city people, especially Texans and Californians.

"We take this class so we don't hurt anyone, including ourselves." He had plenty of stories about people shooting each other while they were out hunting or in their own homes. And we knew of at least two kids our age who'd shot themselves in the feet.

"Carry your firearm pointed at the ground with your finger off the trigger," he said.

He told us to be responsible gun owners and responsible hunters.

"Never aim unless you're gonna kill it," he said. And, "Know what you're aiming at first," and "treat every firearm as if it's loaded."

To pass, we had to shoot .22s and hit the paper target in three places. I could pass a paper and pencil test. Easy. But firing a gun made me nervous. Couldn't focus, couldn't do anything, Mr. Adcock said, and he didn't have time for it.

I couldn't focus on the target because I also had to keep my eye on the meanest boys in class, Bobby, the spitter, and Timmy, who'd chewed tobacco even though he got swats in grade school and suspended in junior high, and who said he'd suffer the punishments to do what he wanted. Bobby and Timmy stood there with loaded .22s.

"Look here, Spacey," Mr. Adcock pulled the little rifle out of my hands. "Right here," he pointed where the cartridge went and loaded it for me. "Better leave the safety on until I can come back here and shoot for you."

The boys laughed. The boys who didn't ever do well in school exceled in Hunter Safety class.

The other kids shot their targets and got to take them home as a Hunter Safety report card.

Mr. Adcock put the rifle in my hands, butted it up against my shoulder, kicked my feet into the right positions and said, "Okay, Spacey, you can't hurt anybody now. So go ahead and shoot and don't take all day."

My target didn't have holes. Mr. Adcock said, "I even looked in the wood around it for holes. You really couldn't hit the broad side of a barn."

My throat tight, I didn't cry.

The other kids were already on the bus when I boarded with Mr. Adcock trailing behind.

Bobby sneered when I walked by, "City girl." The worst insult.

Once we passed Hunter Safety class we could get a deer license for hunting: a one-time license for a particular animal, usually during a particular time of year.

Dave, Mom's boyfriend at that time, took me hunting to help me fill my deer license by either killing the deer for me or helping me shoot it myself. He took me out one morning alone.

He said, "I can get her to kill something," tired of my weakness, my sensitivity. "We'll be back in an hour."

I remember Mom's protest – she had rules about her boyfriends not being alone with us or being in the house when we weren't there. But Dave did what he wanted to do when he wanted to do it – he was the boys varsity head basketball coach, owner of the gun and tackle shop. She relented. He could be imposing. I remember his hands on her, holding her, imprisoning her, bruises on her arms that she said were from other things, which was easy to believe. He could make Mom cry with words. He made me cry.

When I complained in his presence, she said, "You can handle it. You're tough." They laughed.

Why couldn't we have been allies then – Mom and me?

A deer stood on a hill at sunrise, a few miles from our trailer, and I cried at his beauty so Dave knew he had to shoot it. He had good aim. I heard the clack of hoof and crack of bone as the buck tumbled dead, covered in clay and bits of sage. I stopped crying when he died. The worst part over with.

Later Dave moved to Arizona.

Mom then had another gun-toting boyfriend named Vern, a logger and a Seventh-day Adventist and a champion arm-wrestler. I hadn't known Seventh-day Adventists were often vegetarians until decades later because Vern took us hunting and made fun of vegetarianism when Mom brought it up, as she sometimes did for health and money reasons.

He'd say, "Are you a veg-eye-tarian or a hippie?" And laugh through his teeth, his laughter a hee-hee-hiss.

She'd say, "Maybe I am a hippie," a hand on her hip, defiant.

Bald with a gray mustache and beard, Vern wore glasses, plaid shirts, jeans, and work boots. When he dressed up, he wore clean, dark plaid, his best jeans, and cowboy boots, and a scorpion bolo tie with his best belt buckle. He wore baseball caps – the other cowboy hat.

He spent his days logging without the benefit of heavy

equipment. He was a single-saw logger and used his own truck for hauling.

We hunted with Vern and his son, Steve, every season for years.

Steve, a grade younger than Brian, was cheerful, sweet, and funny, with a quiet way about him. I didn't know then what I later learned about that kind of quiet man – violence can be silent, subtle. Steve's friend Scott once ran over a cat when we were older as I watched from the sidewalk, Steve tipping his cap to me as they drove by. I yelled at him later. He said it was just a stray cat and why was I mad anyway – wasn't my cat. He said, "Scott likes to run over cats. It was funny."

One day, a group of us formed a hunting party and drove to a valley about a half hour away, north and east. The valley had open meadows after being logged by Vern and Frank, and Frank's sons, Roy and Paul.

Mom packed a lunch of meatloaf, tortillas, green chiles, salsa, bananas, and hot chocolate in a thermos for later, after the kill, before the drive home.

I wanted to stay in the van, my blue and white home away from home. I watched the scenery – birds, wind, trees, the season, transforming the La Plata Mountains from summer rocky tops to glacial peaks, the highest in my world.

But I had to go with the hunting party. I had a license, and if someone killed my deer and a game warden came along and checked, the real hunter would be in big trouble and so would Mom. Fines we couldn't pay threatened.

We walked out over the crunch of snow, careful not to allow snow over the tops of our boots. We could be out all day.

Brian, Steve, and Vern carried their rifles. Mom carried a jug of water with a big chunk of ice that melted and jangled a soft thud when she climbed over logs or scrambled over boulders or through thick places in the forest.

Steve and Vern and Brian were hunters. Mom and I were flushers.

The hunters went down valley. The flushers walked up along the road a ways and then cut down valley.

We'd meet up with the hunters, probably after the killing of the deer, and I hoped after the dying, too.

Mom said, "Let's sit here awhile and let things get quiet again before we walk on."

We sat in the cold autumn on a log. A creature, probably, I thought, a Tyrannosaurus rex, came crashing down the valley past us, got within twenty feet before we saw it. A bull elk. We sat numb and still as the elk crushed small trees, stomped over larger logs, tearing tree branches along with his rack.

"Doesn't seem like something so loud could survive predators."

I nodded in awe.

I didn't want anyone to shoot him. He was so beautiful and, despite his size and power, afraid.

I hated myself, and I hated that I was part of this.

We heard the explosion of the rifle. Another.

"Probably means they missed. Right?" I said this because I was going to start whining, and I knew how annoying that was for Mom.

"Honey. Stop it. Now. We're doing this now. We're not talking about it."

We kept walking down the valley. I started to wonder if we'd get shot, too.

"They're not going to shoot us in bright orange."

Why did I always feel like such a little kid, even then, helping to hunt deer, killing something so we could have meat in our tacos and our chili that winter instead of just beans? I was supposed to accept all things, to toughen up. I tried.

We met up with the hunters. Dead deer. Not the elk.

Vern gutted the deer, pointing his knife into the rectum and slicing upwards towards the still soft belly.

Mom handed me the liver. Said, "Carry this."

Later, not far away, Vern took the liver from me, put it back into the empty belly of the deer. I rubbed my hands in the snow. Blood on my hands. We gutted and sliced flesh from the deer now hanging in the barn, blood dripping into buckets by the old drum set and boxes from Mom's old life.

That deer died because Vern or Steve or Brian shot it, but he died for me because the license was issued to me – I was a teenager with a deer license, but I still couldn't kill anything.

We didn't hunt for pleasure or sport or to "get back to nature." Hunting – that's how we ate meat then. Meat was a luxury. Venison allowed us that luxury.

The barn smelled of dust and cold, old boxes and unused furniture. We hung the deer carcasses from the back legs, steel rod through hocks, ropes up around rafters. After they were skinned, red muscle and white tendon. White strips of fat and sinew. Bones. We cut off small strips of meat, sliced at it, picking away, picking away to marrow, to grind later for deer burger.

I cried over a deer that had been that morning in tall grass at the edge of the trees along the river. It crossed that river one last time, and the thought of it overwhelmed me – alive, crossing a clear, cold river, then dead. I thought of plucking feathers as a young child and crying over my hen friends, watched them bleed onto the snow hanging by the legs and flapping their wings.

I never meant to sound ungrateful. At school, I never wanted to be fragile.

I heard the labels: "City girl," "Vegetarian," and "Oversensitive." Things you'd never want to be.

I swore to be tougher, to stop crying, to be what Mom and Brian were.

"Please, God, make me stronger."

7. Run

BRIAN SHOT A DEER ON A COLD MORNING BY THE MANCOS River about a mile from our house. I watched his reddened cheeks take that steadying breath, his "Marshall hands," the hands from Mom's side of the family – strong, calloused, not fine fingered and soft like mine and our father's. Brian's shoulder as backstop, not-yet-steady but brave. And then I looked away from him and at the deer and at the low and loud spiraling pop, the deer jerked, a splash of red and a still moment and then a leap. He ran and kept running, disappeared into the tall grass and the trees by the river.

Vern said, "You got him. He's gonna run for awhile. Don't lose him. Go!"

Brian and I ran. At that time, I ran long distances, at least as fast as Brian and sometimes faster. I heard the rush of blood in my ear and the grass swishing by, our running breathing.

Brian said "Shit" under his breath. Even a killer of deer couldn't cuss in front of our mom. She was back behind us, but her ears, like her eyes were sharp. Her temper, too, when we cussed. She washed Brian's mouth out with soap or put hot peppers on his tongue when she had them.

She'd say, "We're not like that."

We had to stop running. The cold took our stamina fast. Our adrenaline evaporated when the guts appeared in front of us, on the bent grass path.

"I'm sure he'll die soon. Don't be hard on yourself," I said. The big sister should aid and comfort.

"Shut up."

"Oh, Brian. I just know it's not feeling pain for much longer."

"Shut up!"

Mom hated the words, "shut up" more than she hated cussing, but she didn't come with us. She let us have this world to ourselves. And she couldn't keep up.

We found him, dead, no light or heat left. A hard death. When Vern, Steve, and Mom got there, we kept words to a minimum. Vern started at the groin and we did what we did with dead deer.

We hauled it back to the van. Brian's kill went better the next time.

The deer lived where we lived. We joked about the tourists with their high powered guns, thinking they're more humane, justifying their back-to-nature hobby. And comparing themselves to us.

"Did you hear about the Texans who shot their jeep to death?"

"Did you hear about the Californians who shot their own dog?"

We joked about it, a sad and angry laughter.

And we hungered.

Our mouths watered when Mom threw some slivers of venison into a pan with the fat she collected on the stovetop.

Boom! The trailer rattled; the windows, the metal outside, the light above the table swayed. Colorado lightning.

The purple and rose of sunset mixed with the slate gray of an arid-land thunderstorm. We stepped outside from time to time to check out the lightning, to watch the massive sky fume. We turned off the television, just in case. Southwest thunderstorms were a better show anyway.

Mom made perfect chili. While it simmered, she made sopapilla dough, rolled it out, cut triangles; each one, about half the size of a paper napkin. Then she heated the oil, watched it; didn't leave it, but looked out at the mighty sky from her kitchen window. I remember her hissing and whispering, sometimes singing, looking out the window as she cooked, as she washed dishes, as she watered plants. Lived much of her life by that window.

She oohed and aahed the same way she did when we watched fireworks in Minnesota during summer visits. She embarrassed us, but inside the trailer and outside of earshot, we laughed. Her happiness begat our happiness. We had an affectionate kind of family. We had space within our family, too – three souls after the father left with his rules, his thundering unpredictability, his stories that made us all feel inferior so he could feel superior. Our mother's rules and chaos and stories of our faults didn't create the same feelings.

Mom sliced off tiny slivers of dough to check the oil temperature. She dropped in triangles, spooned oil over them, turning them over until they puffed and browned.

We ate at the round kitchen table.

"What kinda meat is this, Mama?" I said. She liked when I called her that, it softened her.

"Brain," she said, blowing on her chili. Brian and I looked at each other, stopped in mid-bite. I chose to get it over with – I ate fast, took extra sopapillas. Brian chose humor.

"Chewy," he said and then started his boy-talking grossness.

"Food for thought," Mom said. She held up a a forkful of deer brain. I rolled my eyes. Brian laughed.

"What's this piece thinking?" Brian chewed, faked thoughtfulness, "It's thinking Jenny's eating deer brain, and she's trying not to cry."

"Why does Brian get to say whatever he wants, and if I do, I get in trouble?" I said.

"Because you're older. You have to set a good example," Brian said, stabbing as many brain bits as possible and shoving it all into his mouth.

Thunder kapowed again and the trailer jumped.

"It's true, honey," Mom said. "Also, you're a girl. Girls have to be better."

Brian laughed at that, and brain squeezed between his teeth, his braces. Grandpa paid for them because he said we couldn't have our father's teeth and because our teeth would show poverty. The Marshalls had straight-enough teeth – nothing like our buck teeth, crooked mouthfuls – complicated cycles of poverty and judgment and money and love.

Another roar of thunder caused a gnashing of my teeth.

Mom smiled while Brian went on and on talking about brains.

"I'm eating a happy thought – oh, no, there's the hunter – handsome boy, ouch, I'm dyyyyiiinnggg. Aaaah, this piece isn't dead yet. Mmmm, now it is. Hey, Jenny, you got brains on your shirt."

And I did have brains on my shirt.

Mom said, "It always lands there."

Brian says, "Right on her…"

"Brian!" Mom gave him the look.

"But you're always joking with her and she's always joking about her boobs. So, why…"

"Because you can't."

A crash of sound. We lost the lights. The rain brought a new hue to the landscape and green to the hills, mesas, and mountains. Rainbows arched against the deep slate clouds.

8. Crawl

I STOOD WITH MY FINGER NEAR THE TRIGGER, NOT YET ready to pull it. A deer stood, eating, and pausing to look up every few mouthfuls, waiting to be killed, waiting to feed us. Alone and not wishing to endure another long painful winter, he'd die willingly, he said.

I knew I heard him say this. I believed in the voices of animals. Brian laughed at me when I cried about killing. "Fish don't scream. You ever heard a fish scream?" I told him I had but couldn't prove it.

Brian stood beside me, talked me through how to fire a rifle as if I hadn't known. "Make sure your feet are steady." I balanced, pushed my shoes into the forest floor. "Steady your shoulder, relax. Breathe." Not putting me down, he was being manly and brotherly, wanting my first kill. It would elevate me – I'd be better than just a woman. I'd be a woman who could pull the trigger.

"Breathe. Pull the trigger. Breathe. Pull the trigger." He repeated the prayer of it.

But I didn't pull the trigger.

The deer walked away.

The weakness of me, my gender, confirmed.

And I embraced that weakness because I didn't want to kill, and I didn't have to.

But I had to render meat as redemption.

Later, while cutting venison at the table, deep in some middle-school thought, I felt it, the slice, followed by that blissful moment before pain.

"Mom, Jenny sliced off her finger."

"No, it's just the top of my finger. It's still hanging there." I flipped it up and down, pushed it down into place.

"Jen, step away from the table, you're bleeding all over."

"I think I need a towel."

"You know, Jenny, knives are sharp."

"Ha ha."

"You've gotta hold it above your head, honey."

"She's gonna bleed all over her head now."

A half hour later, it hadn't stopped. Still gushed.

"How long do you think it should take before it stops?"

"Well, do you feel okay?"

"Whatdya mean?"

"Dizzy?"

"She's always dizzy."

"Stop it, Bri."

"No, I'm not dizzy."

"Maybe you should sit down."

"Well, it'll stop by the time we get her to Cortez, so let's just wait it out."

"Yeah, here's another towel. Just hold it up over your head, though."

"Maybe you should press harder."

"I'm pressing. I've been pressing. My fingers are falling asleep."

"Well, that's good, then they won't whine so much."

"Ha ha."

"Well, that's one way to get out of cutting up meat."

In the morning, the middle finger on my left hand had a smile-shaped scar; it mended on its own, like Mom predicted.

I wanted to be popular at school or at least less despised for being fat and for being a know-it-all.

I practiced my back walkover into the splits thousands of times until it flowed like a river.

I'd lost weight and grown another half inch, almost five foot two.

Brian said I was finally pretty and for sure I'd be a cheerleader.

"There's not much competition anyway," Brian said. Mom scanned my belly. I stepped behind the breakfast bar, where I balanced and did leg lifts during *Hee Haw* and *Gomer Pyle*.

Cheerleader tryouts. The only one to do a back walkover into splits. No one else did the splits or any gymnastics.

I didn't make cheerleader.

And I didn't understand why.

Mom said, "There are lots of other things to worry about in the world. You have to learn to accept defeats in life."

"Those other girls didn't do any gymnastics," I cried into the pillow.

"Well, it wasn't about the cheerleading. I think it was a popularity contest."

My throat clogged up and Mom sighed and raised her hands in defeat – her explanation meant something else, and I couldn't see her side of it.

The elementary, junior high, and high schools were all on the same town block. I started my period during a volleyball practice as a freshman. One of the girls ran over to the elementary school building and got my mom, who came over and handed me a pad, hugged me while I sat on the toilet.

"Congratulations. You're a young lady now."

No one laughed in the silent locker room.

I felt lucky and happy and afraid, the last girl in my class to start.

A few girls smiled at me when I came out of the stall, older girls who never smiled at me or who even seemed to notice me.

I walked down the hall on the way to my new high school locker. Groups of kids in corners, leaning on lockers, the usual scenes, we'd moved up to the second floor since the renovation. The school got funding because of its historical significance – the oldest continuous-use school in Colorado.

Only the ghost walked the upper floor until the reconstruction.

Mom and Brian said they heard the ghost during basketball games – the ghost screamed during the games, and they knew it was him and no one else. "Nobody else hears him," Brian said. Mom nodded. They'd always heard the same ghosts.

The principal told us how lucky we were, how grateful we should be to go to high school in this building. He said these were the best four years of our lives, but I thought about the ghost. These were not his best. He hanged himself in the bell tower after the railroad left, but nobody really knew why he'd done it.

I wondered what kind of suffering pushed him into it. Did he do it because he'd never belonged in Mancos or because he felt trapped or was it something else entirely?

On a sunny morning, light filled the trailer. The snow sparkled, soft and a soulful kind of warm – perfect birthday snow.

Mom made cream of wheat with lots of lumps, the way I liked it. This isn't the way to make it, she'd say, but it felt heartier. It tricked what felt like my insatiable hunger.

Mom hugged me, smelling like lilacs and something else very sweet. Her night cream cheek and rough hands. Strong and soft. Everything and impossible.

"Happy birthday, Jeffy." One of her nicknames for me. "I don't want you to expect too much, okay? I can't get you any presents, and I don't know what I can do about a cake, and I'm really so sorry but it might not be much of a birthday."

"It's okay. Did you see the snow?"

Her rose cream cheek against mine, she said, "I'll see you after basketball."

After late practice, which meant the boys teams, both JV and varsity, had the gym first, so the girls teams got it from 8 to 10 p.m. or later. I ran down the dark alley filled with superstitions and ghosts in the quiet darkness.

Tacos. Pink frosting cake. She'd sewn a dress. Patches of color – like a hippie Laura Ingalls would wear. I put it on and spun in the narrow trailer living room.

"Perfect birthday," I sang.

I wrote in my diary and prayed and read the Bible and did my homework and turned fifteen.

WE WERE ALWAYS facing drought – fire on the roadside; parched, dead animals, dust because of Denver and industry and pollution and all of the other people living on the Front Range, east of the Continental Divide. They always had to have enough. There were more of them.

That's how we saw it.

The source of the water started in the highest elevations and some of the water went east into Denver and some flowed west to our side. That Continental Divide splits Colorado in so many ways.

We drove along a dusty road through the piñon and cactus-filled Dolores River Valley: Mormon Tea and hardy juniper. Every-thing salt and thirst and ancient sea.

Mom, Brian, and I visited friends less than twenty miles from our trailer as crows fly. Our friends had to move. A dam was going to be built.

We felt the fear of it – the flooding. The drowning of trees and animals, the filling of burrows.

The archaeologists found what they could find – several Pueblo sites, grave sites, a logging mill. The river would swallow up the past. A museum would be put up. Ghost loggers would live in an underwater town or they'd have to move to the rocky mesa tops. Puebloan ghosts were already accustomed to forced move-ment.

Brian and I took turns riding the friends' donkey.

"Where will the donkey live?" we asked.

No one answered.

We drove away. I wanted Mom to drive faster along the winding road – for once – because I could sense the water backing up
behind the dam.

Brian once dreamed that Mom had staples in her neck.
Woke up yelling. Told her about his dream.

"Whatdya think it means?" Brian said.

"Hmm," Mom blew on her herbal tea, what she called hippie tea.

I didn't hear what they said.

A few months later, her thyroid swelled.

"I have to have an operation," she told us. "I have to stay in
the hospital for a couple of days."

Visions of foster care, cruel adoptive homes, separated from
each other forever. Or having to go live with our father after she
died in the hospital in Cortez. We heard stories about the doctors
in Cortez. It was the place to die, to catch another disease while
you waited hours for treatment for something else. We hadn't
thought much of those stories until that moment.

"I'm going to be fine. Brian, you're going to Tad's and, Jenny,
you're going to the Aspromonte's. And then I'll come home. Don't
worry so much. I need you both to be as mature as I know you can
be."

She had her operation, had half of the thyroid removed. She
stayed in the hospital for a couple of days.

And then she came home.

Mom and Brian sat facing each other one morning. I walked
up, "Why are you looking at each other like that?"

"The dream. That dream I had about the staples," Brian said.
When she removed the bandage, he said that's how she looked in
the dream.

Mom tried not to cry. Brian put his hand on her shoulder
and looked out the window, not into her eyes. Brian shook himself free, patted her shoulder. Walked through the living room,
scooped up the basketball, did a few jump shot rebounds against

the wall above the door the way Dave had taught us to do, and then dribbled outside as the trailer shook.

Mom and Brian dreamed each other's lives.

Mom wore short turquoise necklaces to cover her thyroid scar.

Brian visited our father "because sons needs fathers." It was the eighties, and in California for a while and from time to time, Brian was a different person – a breakdancing boy with long, curly, almost afro-style hair, who listened to heavy metal and wrote articles to someday publish in magazines.

Brian once set a trap at Chicken Creek and caught a possum. Her babies clung to her, some smashed, some not, everything tragic and bloody and ruined. He wanted to be a wild man, a trapper. He wanted to be wild like the rivers, a part of the rivers. He hated dams, ranchers, Californians, and Texans, all of them taking something, using it, buying it, selling it, taming it.

The land was a wildness we lived and wanted more of. The wildness from a source you can't kill. Brian and I used to believe we could be that wild. We believed everything should be that wild.

And we had to navigate it – the wildness, the search, and human need. We wanted wilderness, but it was the agriculture that kept us all fed.

There was a time between when we were wild and when Brian killed that possum and her babies. And there was a time between when the possum died and when Brian's wildness changed. Brian ran traps for ranchers, sometimes for money, and sometimes tanning the hides for a fur swap in Durango, the Four Corners' big city. His conibear traps set in wait for muskrat to keep them from burrowing around head gates and through ditch banks. Everything irrigation controlling the water flow.

But that night when he killed the possum, he came in, told me about the babies and the bloody mother and told me sad things that brave boys don't tell.

And I told him things I didn't tell, that I was afraid of going to hell because every time I prayed to God I saw something that wasn't the Jesus in the stained glass at church. All I thought about were sinful things that wouldn't stop flying into my brain and out of my body, and Brian just listened. I told him that I couldn't understand how prayer always made me think about sex. We laughed, but he also turned serious. He said he knew I was a good girl and not to worry.

III. An American Trailer Trash Republican Childhood

9. Running Mountains

MEAN PATTY, SOMETIMES MY BEST FRIEND, SAID, "YOU GOT to state cuz nobody else in this school wants to run distance and all you do is move your feet slow like this for a mile or two and you win."

I'd qualified for the state track meet, having come in first at the district level.

She slow-motion ran down the hallway, keeping her hands limp like I did when I ran because it kept my shoulders from tightening up. It did look slow.

Cowboy Justin, a football player, snort-laughed, which was funny by itself, and then said, "She does look like that when she gets tired."

Math-smart Tim, with a mean alcoholic father, said, "She's fast, you know. Fast as an Indian."

Patty said, "Shhheeeez, like it's hard to beat a bunch of drunks," and then smiled at Tim. I wished she were ugly then, but she wasn't, and she could say whatever she wanted for a laugh and be mean enough that everyone feared her. Tim's family fostered American Indian children. Claudina stood beside Patty and laughed to hurt me. She was Navajo, a foster child, and Patty's friend for the day. Patty could make us turn against each other and ourselves.

Patty and Tim were rancher royalty, like pioneer royalty, three generations on and could say anything they wanted and no one argued. They all claimed pioneer blood and American Indian blood through a great-great-grandmother so they could be on all sides of a rural argument. Tim once took me out to his truck to show me a fawn he'd skinned, to impress me, he said. He'd give me the hide. "It'll be soft," he said. I cried, though. He stood silent beside me, pulled the tarp back over the fawn. An angry gray wave. "Thought you'd like it," he growled.

Patty was probably right about me not having to run very fast, but not because of the color of a runner's skin like she said, but because there wasn't much competition – very few kids wanted to run distance. I turned to my locker and heard the crackle of static in my hair. Perfect timing.

I heard laughter and Patty said, "Maybe that static makes you faster at going in circles."

Mom said I won because of God. She wanted me to be humble, "God is generous with you. Always remember that winning is God's glory, not yours," she said whenever I won or placed well at a meet, but my failures were my own. Mom's religion, like her temperament and her affection, ebbed and flowed. A tide in a high desert on the reservation or an avalanche in a mountain town. We traveled hours to track meets in the Four Corners area. During track season, our lives rose higher and felt hotter and colder. The chance of a college scholarship if it was God's plan.

The Oreos in my pack were there for the ride back, three hundred miles.

"It'll be a reward," Mom said, because she rarely bought junk food.

She said, "Don't eat them until after. You know how you get." I couldn't stop once I started, my own uncontrollable tide.

She packed them into the backpack, kissed me on the crown of the head, and said, "You can do anything you put your mind to."

She hugged me and said, "You're as fast as an Indian, just remember that." That comparison gave me strength and fueled my desire to belong, my desire for many kin, and lasted just long enough until I turned soft again and knew I didn't belong.

I felt deep pressure for this track meet. We got a town send-off – dozens of people gathered around the rented van, driven by Mr. Willburn, sweeter than Mr. Adcock. He'd drive us through the state of Colorado to get there, from one corner to the other, north then east across the divide.

As we left, a man said, "You better bring a medal home, little girl."

Mom said, "You be gracious. It's not all about you, and for goodness' sake don't cry," when I told her that I was afraid of letting everyone down.

Alone in a motel room in Denver – I was the only girl to make it to the state meet – I held my cleats to my chest, Tammy's shoes. She was the daughter of the town journalist. The shoes had a sort of magic because Tammy shared them with others – so many of us couldn't afford our own. We applied our successes to them, feeling mightier instead of poorer. I changed to short spikes for the fancy rubberized track. Mancos High School didn't have a track. For a 400-meter run, we ran about one and a half times around the football field in a well-worn path.

I focused on the shoes so I could ignore the Oreos.

I prayed, "Please God, let me win a medal. Please God."

I prayed and fell asleep and dreamed that the Sleeping Ute Mountain on the Ute Mountain Reservation, southeast of Cortez, had risen according to the legend we'd learned on the playground to kill all the white people. Patty drove a pioneer wagon, whipping the four horses of the apocalypse, in Biblical colors – red, black, white, and pale, but she didn't see the Walking Ute Mountain up behind her, walking toward her. I thought it was funny until I heard God yell and I woke up to the alarm.

Before I left the room, I noticed the painting above my bed.

An American Indian rode a painted pony, both of them, heads bent and leaning into the wind, the sky in the painting was lightning and shades of red in the distance.

I cried until the coach banged on the door and said, "It's time."

God and I got a third-place medal in the 2-mile that day.

I offered the Oreos to the boys in the van, but they had plenty of their own food. I ate the cookies and wanted more.

Later, when the school year ended, I walked out of the trailer on a June day, still thin from track season.

I wore a bikini – navy blue with tiny white polka dots – first time I'd ever worn a bikini.

Mom worked the garden, chucking rocks over the barbed wire.

I'd had another bad night. Bored and lonely while Mom worked her waitressing job at the Millwood Junction, I'd tried to make cookies without butter or eggs or banana or oil. I used milk and flour.

"Thanks for trying," Brian said. "For cookies without butter or eggs, they're really good," but he didn't eat any.

Mom looked up at me, "You've gained a couple of pounds."

I put my hands to my belly, trying to cover it.

She was right. That morning, the scale said that I weighed ninety-two pounds. Not too skinny for a five-foot-two inch girl, but thin enough, especially for someone who used to be chubby and who would be chubby again, more than chubby.

"Yeah, I guess," I said.

"Yeah, I guess," she repeated, her tone sarcasm and daggers.

She fit that label "normal." She didn't have the battle I had with my expanding, shrinking, expanding body.

Maybe she was mad because I used up the milk she'd been saving for our meals.

Maybe she was mad because she'd spent money on a bikini only to see me with a puffy stomach.

Maybe she was mad because she couldn't decide whether it was better for us to be hungry and me to be thin enough to pass for normal or better for us to have enough food and me blimp up and float away, but my weight didn't reflect whether we had money or not.

Next day, she told me I couldn't wear my favorite sweater – too tight, try something looser.

Brian told me not to drink water when I was thirsty. It would make me weaker and thirstier. He told me to drink water when I was eating to fill me up.

He told me to eat things in a different order and a different way so that I wouldn't be so hungry.

During track season, he told me not to drink water when I ran, and not right after because I'd just want more water. I'd start to need it more.

"You gotta need less. If you give yourself less, you'll need less. You'll be tougher."

A stack of diet books and exercise tapes sat piled on Mom's nightstand that was also the coffee table where she slept in the living room – Richard Simmons, Weight Watchers, aerobics with Jane Fonda, her public image redeemed after protesting against the Vietnam War, and there was Helen Gurley Brown and a pile of Cosmo magazines.

Brian said Mom's butt was too big, but to me, she was tiny except for the soft belly where my brother and I had been.

I wrote in my diary, "I feel depressed about my weight – do something!" and "God gives me everything and what do I do?"

Brian, Mom, and the rest of our extended family poked fun at my fat, my constant battle with fat, my belly, my sometimes round belly.

My flesh, a universe, I said, "I expand and contract," to make people laugh, to divert them from criticizing my weight. There was safety in the solitude of excess flesh, and there was comfort in food. I watched the sun in its vast arc, as thunderclouds gathered and the lightning flashed across the world. I hungered to understand. I wanted to fill that hunger and the other hunger that would be a sin to feed, and I fed it with food because it was all I could think to do. In that small town in the middle of an expanse between one place and somewhere else, there wasn't much to do. I wanted my mother to understand my hunger, but I couldn't understand it either.

My breasts grew large even when I was thin. I joked about my breasts, laughing before others, putting people at ease with judgment, theirs and my own.

Mom said, "I hope you take this the right way. I bought you a shirt." It said, "Flat is beautiful." We laughed at the word stretched across my breasts.

Every track season, I had that five pounds, that ten pounds, to lose for running long distances.

"You have heart," my coach said, "It makes up for what you don't have."

Mom said, "You need a support bra," and she let me know about the expense. "You have to be modest."

Mondays I started new diets, which meant feeling hungry as much as possible because weight loss only happened through hunger. I ignored the dizziness with small rituals – writing food lists, weighing myself, counting to distract myself: 1, 2, 3, 4, 4, 3, 2, 1, 1, 2, 3, 3, 2, 1, 2, 2, 1, 1, etc.

Mom told me her mother was bone thin when she died. When she told me this, she looked off into the sky, the blue of her eyes remained dry. She held her emotions in check for our sake as often as she could. She believed adult sadness upset children too much and so should be contained.

"People said that she looked so good because she was thin," Mom said. "But she was dying – people become thin while they're dying. She'd been curvier and rounder during most of her life. You're more like her than I am."

Mom paused, "Do you understand what that means?"

Unsure, I said yes.

"You do? What does it mean?"

"Um…"

"No, you don't understand. You can't understand. It means people thought it was more important that she be thin than that she live."

"Yeah. So, it doesn't matter what you weigh," I said, hopeful and excited, thinking I understood.

"Well," she said, "that's not exactly what I meant. You're like her. You look like her, and you're busty like her." I sensed an edge. Some thought or fear I didn't want to touch.

She turned to the mirror, adjusted her long denim skirt, belted over a sweater. "Do you think this makes me look – well, too bunchy?"

"You could never look bunchy," I said. She smiled.

I sat on my bed ashamed, bunchy, busty, and too much.

And still I wanted more. I always wanted more.

10. Sex Education

I'D BEEN TO A MOVIE WITH MIKE, AND EVEN THOUGH HIS mom and my mom were there, and also our siblings, it was sort of like a date. At a football game with David, I drank my first Diet Pepsi under the bleachers – first because Mom hated sodas – and that was sort of like a date, too. I went to the homecoming dance on my first real date with Huey when I was a freshman and he was a junior. He wore a powder-blue western-style jacket with white piping, scorpion bolo tie, and shiny cowboy boots. He had an eagle feather in his cowboy hat – legal for him as an American Indian. Neils asked me to be his girlfriend. He'd passed me a note during math, and I knew how much he loved math, but he was Mormon.

Mom and I sat on the steps, careful of splinters and small puddles, and I told her how I thought life could be made to be fair, how it could be good for everyone. I wanted to prove my heart's sweetness and wisdom.

"I don't want to be a Mormon," I said during one of those out-of-the-blue-teen-to-mother philosophy sessions. It always felt like there was a threat, an invisible pressure to become Mormon in the land of the Latter Day Saints.

"I like Mormons," she said, the corners of her lips turned upward, eyes wide.

"Mom, you told me you think women should have a right to divorce, that it should be easier to divorce and harder to marry, that women shouldn't have to have so many children. Just the other day, you told me this."

"Mormons celebrate birthdays."

I'd forgotten hers the day before, and she was still hurting.

"The Wayburns. Mom. They're polygamists. Everyone knows that."

"You shouldn't make fun of the Wayburns. It's not easy to get rid of a head lice problem. I'd just like a card on my birthday."

I said, "I'm not making fun of the head lice. I'm not making fun of them being poor either or any of the other reasons people make fun of them. Everybody here's poor. We're poor. I'm talking about Mormons, Mom. Is it right that they make women have so many babies? Is it right that they foster Indian kids because they don't want them to be too Indian?"

"That's not the way of it. Those are loving homes, and we are not poor," she said.

"It's pretty much the way of it," I said. I kept talking back and could feel the temperature between us rise.

"The point is that you always forget to give me a birthday card until you're reminded. They," she said in a long syllabled accusation, "celebrate family."

I stopped talking to her then, unable to articulate my thoughts, unable to reach across the divide I felt, and I'd hurt her feelings. I'd forgotten her birthday card. We didn't have the kind of family she was talking about, and she didn't want that kind of family. We lived far from family. Her brother's wife, our Aunt Barb, had said, "I wouldn't divorce without a very good reason. I'm not that kind of person." She and our uncle had named their youngest son after our father.

On a different day, same step, I said, "Joseph Smith created a whole new religion based on the idea that white people had been in America before and that the Indians and white people had lived together before, but then the white people all died out and left this religion, etched into tablets and buried it all for the return of the white people to America."

She shook her head, whisper-hissed. "Where do you get this?"

"It's true, Mom, so I could write a religion." She laughed and wondered if I was kidding, but I went on. "I'd make sure women were equal to men and could have multiple husbands if they wanted to."

Mom said, "I don't want even one husband."

We laughed as the sun set over the chalk-colored hills and Mesa Verde in the distance and the mountains behind us became dark giants.

"What are you laughing about," Brian wanted to know, his hair ruffled on his head, no t-shirt over his rib-ragged chest.

"Oh, nothing," Mom said. She shushed me with her gaze.

That was one of those conversations not for Brian's ears.

Later, Mom said, "You can have children without being married. If you get married because you're pregnant, you're making two mistakes instead of one." But she said, "You, of course, don't have to worry about any of that yet. Not until you're much older."

When I told her there were girls in town having sex already, she said, "Well, that couldn't be true." And then she said, "If they are, they'll ruin their reputations." She said that people would say, "They have hinges on their heels," and she didn't disagree. She said, "If you act like them, I'll disown you."

I had to navigate ever more complex mixed messages.

I woke up one morning to find mean and wiry Norma shaking my shoulder hard, digging her fingernails in.

"Get up, lazy!" Someone else laughed. Sharon, a senior, daughter of the English teacher and the science teacher, my mother's coworkers.

These girls had never been in our trailer before.

"What's..."

"You'll see."

I got out of bed and they screamed with laughter because I wore a nightgown, torn in many places, including along the top seam, so that one of my boobs stuck out.

"You have to wear that nightgown," they said when I reached for a pair of jeans on the floor.

"No. I'm not doing this," I said, but Norma grabbed my arm, dug those fingernails in deeper than before. Junior. Basketball starting lineup and fang-mean.

"You have to. Your mom said."

Norma pulled me past Brian's closed door.

I willed myself to have a sense of humor, but it didn't work out.

"Mom!" I pleaded as they dragged me past her.

Her daughter about to go into that Christian town with a breast showing, she had a pained look in her eyes.

"I almost told you to wear a t-shirt or something last night, but I didn't want you to know about the surprise."

"The surprise!" I almost cried.

They led me to their car. Mom made an exception to her rule about my never being allowed to get into other teenagers' cars.

It was a dry, cold, icy morning. Norma threw snow into my jacket before she sat down next to me and told Susan, "We got the best one."

She told me to take off my glasses. I cradled them, protective. They'd help me survive the trial coming next, then she blindfolded me.

I couldn't imagine why Mom let this to happen, but anger kept me from crying.

We drove for only a few minutes, of course – the town was so small – and then Norma pulled me across icy pavement. I fell, scraped my knee. Norma demon-laughed harder than ever as she pushed me along. I heard a crow, strained to see through my blindfold, felt pavement, stairs, heard doors, felt tile.

Norma removed the blindfold, and I put my glasses back on.

We stood in the basement of the Mormon temple that doubled as the Masonic Lodge – so much shared hierarchy, so many symbols.

The girls from my class were there except two – the new girls from the city with scientist and journalist parents. Patty, Kallie, Connie, Becky, Donna, Catherine, and Wendy (we went to the same church). Girls from the next class younger – Janet and Rose, the girl with a wall of belts as parenting weapons.

"Take off your jacket," Norma pulled at my jean jacket as I tried to keep my nightgown holes pinched together, but there were too many to handle.

Our captors didn't allow us to talk to each other.

Connie groaned. Norma laughed at her and made her do push-ups.

The older girls herded us up the stairwell and into a small room where they stopped us at a heavy dark door.

They took Kallie away first. We waited. Silent. No screams, but that didn't make me feel better.

I thought about Mom. I knew she loved me. She wanted me to be tougher, though. Stronger. She'd spanked my brother and me often enough. Her violence I could endure, knowing more of her existed on the other side of it. Her violence was a weapon, but it also was an artifact of her weakness and exhaustion and ignorance. But I feared the pain inflicted by other people.

Fang-mean Norma and coward Susan took the other girls one at a time.

When it was my turn, Norma threw a sweater at me. I buttoned every last button and breathed relief.

We walked through the door into a small room with two doors on one wall. She knocked on the one on the right, the door opened and Paula said, "Who requests entry?" as if she couldn't see me and as if we didn't live in a small town where we knew even the names of stray cats.

A giant Bible rested on a dark wood table in the center of the room, a light shining on it from the ceiling.

Paula, the Drill Leader – "Sister Drill Leader" put out her arm out for me to hold and led me to the first station, where Susan, an older girl, said, "Worthy Advisor, I beg to serve you."

Lori said, "Be advised, and through you, the Sister of Faith, who is seated near the altar, the Sister of Hope, who is seated in the South, and the Sister of Charity who is seated in the North, that this Assembly of the Order of the Rainbow is about to be opened."

There was a lot of bowing, asking for permission, commands given and carried out.

The Confidential Observer informed the Outer Observer that "the doors of this Assembly are now to be closed and the assembly will begin its study of True Womanhood."

The American flag was presented and we said the Pledge of Allegiance.

The Bible was opened, "That its white light may penetrate the heart of every member of this Assembly."

White, the Virgin color, we were told, was the symbol of True Womanhood.

The Mother Advisor, Brenda's Mom, and the Worthy Advisor, Mean Norma, stood at the front of the room. They ordered us to keep silent about everything we experienced.

Afterward, we ate pancakes in the basement and the older girls told us how much fun we'd have as Rainbow Girls.

Most of us joined. Mom explained that I had a right to join and couldn't be denied because her father was a Mason.

We took solemn oaths and memorized lines and earned pins.

We prayed, "Bless the Girlhood of our Nation; may it feel and know its responsibilities and especially may it have Thy divine guidance through the early years of life. Bless, we pray Thee, the great Masonic Fraternity; bless the Order of the Eastern Star; bless our Masonic home and the children therein; keep us from evil; teach us reverence, teach us to give to Thee each day a portion of our time. Then we shall have Victory, and praise Thee forever. Amen."

Every night, we were to read Genesis, Chapter 9 and leave it open by our beds.

We kept secrets and performed rituals and learned that our highest and greatest good was to become soft-spoken and subtle and patriotic, good mothers, loyal wives.

Being a girl, a young woman meant being kind and gentle and virginal.

Virginity, in fact, should be held as the most precious thing about us. We were to guard it with our lives, should it come down to that.

A friend asked me, "Can you get pregnant if you only get really, really close to having sex, but his thing doesn't actually go into your you-know?"

We huddled by our locker, voices in whispers to protect her from the small town ears and from her rancher dad, strict and mean and powerful

"I don't think so," I said.

"Are you sure?"

"Well, are you pregnant?"

"I don't think so."

We'd grown up around animals, but the biology of animals didn't give us the information we needed about ourselves.

"Well, have you had your period?"

"Periods don't always come when they're supposed to, but I didn't have sex." She paused, "Not actually." Her curly brown hair bounced as she trembled.

I said, "I guess I just don't know if you can get pregnant any other way besides actually having sex," but I thought about God impregnating Mary.

She said, "Well, I'm not pregnant. I couldn't be." She paused again, "Besides, isn't it true that you can only get pregnant if you're married?"

"No. I mean. I don't know. No, you can pregnant if you're not married." I paused, confused, "Pretty sure."

"I can't talk to my mom. She'd kill me for getting that close." Her brows tilted together in fear.

"Yeah." I knew her mom. She was almost as strict as mine, according to Patty, who always talked about the strict moms that way – the moms who enforced bedtimes through high school, the moms who let you bear the consequences when a teacher got mad at your behavior or you got a bad grade even when unjust things happened leading up to them.

"Well, don't tell anybody I almost had sex."

"I won't," I said. "But no one would believe me anyway."

"About me not having sex?"

"No one would believe you got close to having sex or that you had sex, and no one would believe you were pregnant or even talked about it."

"Yeah?" She smiled, eyes wide. She radiated goodness. She made me smile, too.

"You are sweet and good and everybody knows your dad would kill you."

"Yeah." She looked relieved. She had shelter from gossip, cruel as her father could be.

"You're the girl my mom's always comparing every other girl to," I followed a seam of perfect hand-sewn stitches in her blouse. She sure could sew.

"Oh." She slouched for a second before returning to her usual perfect posture.

"Yeah."

She looked sad again. "Sorry."

"It's okay." I knew I should stop talking.

"Well, I gotta get to class."

"Me too."

We sat together in class that hour as if we'd never had that conversation. So much could change the course of our lives.

I SLEPT WITH my door open. In case. In case I needed to escape or my mom needed to save me. There were many ways for the devil to enter a room.

I prayed to be good in thought, word, and deed.

When I prayed, I closed my eyes on my back because I had a bunk bed and didn't want to kneel and then climb up afterward. I put my hands flat on the bed, palms down. I didn't want my hands to wander. It seemed wrong – no, more than that really – to touch some other part of my body, any other part with my hands while trying to get the attention of God.

Brian, asleep in the room next to mine, his door always closed was more into barricades and strongholds for defense.

I believed in symbols and submission and escape. I crossed myself when I finished praying for goodness and security, but Brian was also right about borders – a good barricade could be a good defense. I wrapped the blankets closer to my neck – vampires couldn't chew through blankets. No one confirmed this, but I reasoned this had to be true. In the movies, vampires went for bare necks.

The wind howled, the trailer rocked. I heard things blowing around outside. There was a smell of possum coming up through the register.

I filled up with fear because I couldn't pray without God transforming. I tried to envision His face, the way I'd been taught to think of it – a blur of light, a haloed hint of light brown hair, but it was like stone and smoke, smudged. I couldn't envision God with his robes on still, male and therefore with male anatomy – that's what made him King of All. I didn't want to think about his male anatomy, but the more I tried not to imagine it, the more I imagined it.

I confessed. But not to that. I confessed to loss of faith, which was better than loss of propriety.

Jesus was no help. Covered with cloth, bleeding in gold paint above my bed, hanging on his cross, His troubles were far greater than mine could ever be. I wanted to have made that death of His meaningful – the reason He died for me, for my soul, for all of us and I failed Him time and again.

I cried, desperate.

My hands wandered, comforting against my skin.

I knew I would be going to hell.

The wind thinned the trailer walls, cans smashed into the trailer and rolled down the alley, tossed along the stones and rock-hard ruts. I became aware that metal and blankets and intentions wouldn't protect me from the devil or from God.

Jesus and I were alone.

I touched his feet and curled into a ball, becoming a smaller target for the lightning I knew was headed my way to blast me into hell.

I sang "The Gambler" because it always made me feel better, even though it was such sadness or maybe because it was such sadness.

And I spiraled away from God.

I practiced my poker face in the dark.

11. Small Town Dreams

PATTY HAD A MESSAGE FOR ME – SHE SAID THAT PAUL liked me. I liked his smooth and perfect skin, thick black hair with gray-blue-hazel eyes. He played every sport, too – football, basketball, and track, like most Mancos kids, but he was good at everything.

We met by the gym on the new ramp. People grumbled about the money spent on it, but it was the law that schools be accessible for everyone. We paced the hall, running our hands along the smooth, new, metal handrail.

We said hello and stood looking outside until we got the courage to turn face to face.

Paul said, "I like Chris, but I like you more." Chris, new from California, would do it with him, he said. "I'd rather be with you, but I need to know that we'll do it."

"I don't know," I said. Sin. I feared it. He and I were religious, our families were church-going. We had the same God, our services spoke the same words. The pope and confession were the differences between him and me, but sin, I knew, had to be the same.

"We don't have to do it right away," he said. "But Chris said she'll do it soon."

I looked out at Menefee Mesa with its rock outcropping standing sharp and heavy over the south border of the valley.

"I don't want God to hate me."

"If we have sex, we'll get married someday."

I was almost sixteen. I wanted a boy to love me.

I wrote in my diary, "Paul's so nice."

Basketball was part religion – that we had in common with every other real place in the universe. The other girls and I stood on the baseline of the basketball court. Sweat, perfume, the scent of soap and emotion. Shoulders back, opening the lungs for sweet air and a moment of rest.

We were almost done, almost free of basketball practice, almost free of the coach and his judgment and cruel ways.

"Line it up," he shouted.

"Killers until I say stop," he said. "Stay together." He didn't mean for the fast girls to slow down. He meant for the slower girls to keep up.

We ran from the baseline to the free-throw line and back, to the center and back, to the other free throw and back, full court and back.

One killer completed. Repeat.

After practice, we walked out into the cold clear night.

When I got to the alley, I ran along the rutted, deep dark ground aiming for the shadow of the barn and the light from the kitchen shining into the alley – when I hit that light, I knew I'd be safe from ghosts, vampires, demons, and dogs. I prayed that I wouldn't twist an ankle. More than that, I kept the prayer at the front of my mind should it be necessary to face down a vampire, "In the name of the Father, Son and Holy Ghost…"

And I ran faster and faster to Mom's kitchen light.

Friday night basketball games. The junior varsity girls played first, then the JV boys, then the varsity girls, then the big game, the most-valued game – the varsity boys.

I played guard because of my height. The coach wished for me to be fast or technical. His wish remained unfulfilled. Sometimes, I made a miracle shot or two. From time to time, Jesus sank my free throws. I played every season because sports covered my many failings, my gathering sins, and held my place in the community.

Every fall, the coach said to me, "You're going out for the team, right? You know we need your leadership." I wanted that. So much, I wanted that.

Coach said, "It's important to have some experience on the bench."

I had lots of that, so we laughed.

Short but strong, Paul played forward for the varsity team. Everyone said that he looked like a Mexican-American version of John Elway, the most beloved Colorado football Jesus – the Denver Broncos' quarterback.

Saturday nights, when we didn't have a football or basketball game, Paul picked me up in his Toyota truck and took me to the P&D. He played Donkey Kong and Asteroids while I watched or walked the convenience store aisles.

I cheered for him, "Oh, you're doing good. What level are you on?" as if I could tell. I started conversations.

He said, "Shut up. I'm trying to play." A lump formed in my throat.

His best friend, Mike, said, "Oh, she's gonna cry." Paul didn't talk to Mike for a few months because Mike called Paul a "wetback." Mike apologized and promised he'd never say anything like that again. Paul said he'd never forgive him, but they'd always be best friends as long as Mike kept his word. They passed the spit can between them.

Most of the time I didn't cry.

When Paul finished playing his games, he said, "Let's go."

Mike smiled at Paul, looked at me, jerked his chin up at me, half smiling, walked out to his own truck.

Paul drove to the alley behind the barn where we were invisible to sin, the trailer, and my mom.

I'd turned sixteen and he'd turned seventeen.

I was unwilling to die for my virginity, as it turned out.

I didn't really want to have sex, which meant the biblical definition – his penis inside my vagina – the other things we didn't see as sex, didn't admit to doing. I'd made an agreement, a promise, to Paul to do them so he'd be my boyfriend. Since the beginning, I'd known it was inevitable, but I'd also thought that somehow I could get out of it. Women were supposed to save men from themselves. Women were supposed to be worthy of waiting for. A good woman was the prize of becoming a married man, and I believed all that. And I'd been raised to keep a promise when I made it. Raised by a woman who'd been disappointed by the breaking of promises, spoken and inferred.

We parked in the alley beside the barn where we hung deer to bleed. It was time.

He said, "We have to hurry. I have to get up early to go work with my dad." He logged with his father sometimes.

I LAID BACK on the seat of his mother's Chevy four-door sedan and he pushed his way into me.

I looked into his eyes in the small darkness between us, the gentleness I saw didn't match the pain I felt. I fell into it, seeking relief and to be good, redeemed by Paul's affection for me.

"Hurry. Finish. No, go slow. It hurts," I said.

I watched the stars, the Perseids, and satellites; I willed them to take my mind off the pain and to hide me from God.

I cried when he pulled away from me, hell-bound then, for sure, even though I hadn't used birth control and so hadn't intended to sin. Surely, God took intention into account.

"It'll be okay. We'll get married," he said.

I hid my underwear in the dresser until I had a period and then I lumped it in with the rest of my laundry. I never got the hang of how to bleed without bleeding on everything. Grace, Mom said, can take a long time.

For months, we parked behind the barn.

Sin shamed us into silence. Paul said, "Don't tell anyone about what we do," and shame required a facade. "I don't want any of the guys to know."

As time passed, he got more and more jealous, emotional, and controlling.

"I don't want you to spend so much time with Britt," he said. "I don't like her family – they think they're better than the rest of us."

He wanted me to spend my extra time with him.

At school, he stayed close by, didn't leave me alone. He was eighteen. I was seventeen. He put his hands down my pants while we rode the school bus past the grassy ranch lands of the Mancos Valley through the sage-filled hills to the Vocational-Technical school, past the Mesa Verde entrance, partway to Cortez. I didn't want him to, afraid of being caught, but he said, "I'll tell everybody about you," so he did what he did, and I didn't stop him. Humiliated either way.

I believed what I'd been told, that I was ruined. I thought about Bible verses and high school hallway taboos and steeped myself in this grief.

I told Mom that sometimes Paul was mean to me but didn't mention the specifics. I didn't want to tell her about his digging, hurting fingers, the way he used his body even when I said no to certain things or wanted to say no but knew he wouldn't hear it anyway, and a smaller thing: the names – slut, bitch, tease. His phrases, "I'm just joking" and "That doesn't hurt you," and his ever-cruel hands, not leaving marks. Subtle.

"He's just a teenager, honey," she said. "He'll grow out of it. How bad could it be?"

"You're too sensitive," she said. "Everyone knows that."

"He can't really hurt you anyway," she said. "Unless you put yourself in a situation."

Paul and I parked out at Jackson Lake, a reservoir like so many Colorado lakes. Dammed up, made for cattle. In the warmer months, we had sex in the bed of his truck. I watched the trees sway in the breeze above him while I held his strong back. In the winter, we had sex on the wide truck seat. I held onto the back of the seat and looked past his gray-blue-hazel eyes out the back window at the shadows of the forest until the windows fogged over and ice formed. And sometimes I felt so good and thought I could stay there in the steaming truck in the snowy forest forever. We'd have beautiful children, I knew.

We never used birth control.

I brought it up once.

"I can't feel anything with a rubber," he said.

"We've never used a rubber," I said. "So, how do you know?"

He said he just did.

He pulled out just before coming. I felt for when he was close, ready to push him away, but he always knew when he would.

The truck got stuck in the deep snow one winter night.

"It's better for you to go over there," he said. "You're white."

I walked to the big house there, knocked on the door. Had to knock a few times.

A man finally answered. Angry.

"Hi," I said, suddenly afraid.

"Yeah?"

"My boyfriend's truck is stuck out here."

"What were you doing out there this time of night?" When I didn't answer in words, he said, "You know, little girl, we've been pulling people outta here all day long. I'm eating my dinner now. I'm gonna finish and I might or might not come out there to help you."

Slammed the door shut.

I walked back. Said, "I don't think he's gonna come out here. We might need to start walking."

He said, "You're so stupid."

We sat in silence for hours, turning the engine on when it got really cold, but keeping a mind not to run out of gas.

The man finally came out and got Paul's truck out of the snow.

I walked into the trailer three hours after my curfew.

Mom didn't speak to me.

"Mom, Paul's truck got stuck out at Jackson Lake." I kissed her goodnight. I missed her cheek, got her ear.

She said, "Oh, I can see you've got a great bedside manner."

She was angry and trying to hurt me, shame me, to raise me up right, but also because she was afraid.

I wrote in my diary "Praise God for periods."

I went to bed, but didn't sleep. My feet were so cold.

That night I dreamed my feet were stuck in the mud of a drained Jackson Lake, but then the water started rising and freezing. I drowned under blocks of Jackson Lake ice and they were about to blow it all up because the suckerfish invaded again. I woke up when I heard a man say, "Let's restock it with native trout."

In the autumn of my senior year, homecoming happened again, the way it had in Mancos since the narrow gauge train days. The time of the bonfire and the burning of the enemy's mascot in effigy, the queen and her attendants, the football game and the dance.

My childhood dream of becoming a princess was finally granted. The football team voted to decide which girl would be queen and which two would be attendants. Five girls remained in our class after attrition from pregnancy and poverty and needing to take care of family in other places, on reservations and back in the South. Patty and I got the same number of votes and Wendy got the most.

Mom said, "That's appropriate because Wendy is the nicest of the three."

Paul told me I couldn't be in the homecoming ceremony because I'd have to kiss one of the football players.

I said, "Well, you kissed Chris Peterson last homecoming when you were a captain of the football team."

"That's different," he said. "Because I wasn't a girl kissing a guy. If you kiss another guy, he'll get the wrong idea. He'll think he can do other things with you."

"Everyone will be watching," I said, "I doubt that he'll just jump me, right there in front of God and everybody."

"No. But after the game," Paul said.

"You'll be here after the game. Just like always," I said.

But he was going to a party in Cortez, where the parties were better because there weren't high school kids. I told him I'd be going to homecoming and I'd kiss someone else during halftime.

His lips tightened, his jaw set, and his eyes narrowed. "If you kiss somebody else, I'll break up with you," he said through his teeth.

"That's not fair."

"Life isn't fair."

At homecoming, during halftime, I kissed Mustache Mike, who went home right after the game so that Paul wouldn't have to beat him up.

Paul's mom made tortillas thick and warm because I liked them so much when I went to their trailer by the river.

"Even though this isn't the way to make them," she frowned over them – tortillas should be thin, she told me.

Paul's grandma made everything the traditional way, including the lamb and everything from the lamb. Paul and I hated the eyeballs.

When our family killed a deer, we put the eyeballs outside for critters to scream over – the birds, the cats, raccoons, and dogs, and the coyotes in the night. I heard them through the trailer floor, sniffing the leftover blood. Every living thing in Mancos had deer blood in their veins.

Paul's dad hugged me, papa bear-like, *"Que bonita, m'ija."* He smelled like sweat, tree sap, and tobacco. He logged with Mom's boyfriend, Vern.

Paul's cousin said, "Hey, prima," whenever he saw me in school.

Paul's father, hard-working and generous with his strong back, helped anybody who asked. No one ever messed with him because he was afraid of no one and nothing. He made jokes about Mexicans and American Indians and called people things we weren't to repeat.

Mom said, "He makes jokes about loose women," and, "I shouldn't tell you this, but Dolores tells me her husband hits her, but you're not to tell anyone." I wanted to tell Mom he wasn't the only one, that she wasn't the only one – that it had nothing to do with culture, like Mom said, but with sex, our sex, our being female, and if it was about culture, it wasn't just one culture, it was all of them maybe, but it was too complicated. I couldn't explain.

I wanted to tell her about every girl I knew who was being hurt – Sherri and Pam and their boyfriends who laughed at school, in that gauntlet of a hallway, about the bruises their boyfriends inflicted, the girls showing them off, their faces tough. I wanted to tell her about Rose, in the house across the highway, whom I could hear screaming sometimes, and also, that being hit wasn't the only way to be hurt. I wanted her to help me articulate what I desired – mercy in all relationships, but it wasn't possible.

But I didn't tell anyone what Mom told me about Paul's mother, not even Paul.

Mom told me Dolores said divorce was for cowards.

A good woman, Dolores told her, believes in the power of love and goodness and food to make things work out, to help them survive anything and everything. A good woman believed bravery and goodness to be more important than flesh.

I wanted to believe in that mythology, too, or rather I meant to. I wanted to be that good, that brave and loving. I prayed, begging God to recreate me in every way and in every task. But I'd forget and then want a different kind of goodness, something I couldn't name.

When I asked Mom to teach me to cook, she said, "You don't need to know how to do this. Cooking is easy. Anyone can learn. Besides, we don't have the money to spare to give you cooking lessons if things don't go well. You won't have to learn the way a wife cooks. I can't imagine you married."

I cried over all of that and started falling apart. I stopped running, stopped wearing makeup, stopped curling my hair, and I stopped reading books.

"You're so sensitive," Mom said, as she tried to soothe me later. "You take things the wrong way. You're supposed to be more."

She struggled, too – some Sundays she didn't get out of bed.

She worked so hard, she said, and no one helped her. "Go outside," she said. "Find something to do."

She splurged one weekend and rented a VCR from the kiosk at the gas station. We watched *Conan the Barbarian* with Arnold Schwarzenegger. Conan, toughened by a childhood of sleeping in the snow, battled a giant serpent while seeking vengeance for his mother's beheading. He wouldn't cry, so his friend cried for him. Conan used his god's name, not in vain, but in awe and rage. "Crom," he'd say, when he struck down his enemies or when he saw something he couldn't explain.

We laughed and cried and repeated the line.

The next brilliant lightning storm that lit the valley's slate sky, Mom turned to me and said, "Crom."

She said, "Sometimes we just need a story."

PAUL SAID, "OUR first child's name will be Hector Macho Camacho Gonzales – a great boxer."

I said, "No. Please." I imagined my child with bruises, giving bruises. Fighting. The violence.

He said, "What's wrong with that? It's not like you get to name the children anyway. The wife doesn't get to name the babies."

I thought about cowboy Justin and tough, wayward Kallie and the bruises he left on her arms. She said they were everywhere. Kallie, the daughter of a Mormon bishop left as a sophomore and came back different. She'd always been strong, but when she returned, no pain was too much for her to bear. The Latter Day Saints required her to be ready for anything. She was a monster in volleyball and basketball.

I wasn't strong like any of the women I knew. I couldn't do what they could do.

I started a new diet, dreamed of running a five-minute mile, seeking to become beautiful enough, strong-enough, something-enough to negotiate my life, to have the power to name babies I'd push into the world.

MAYBE PAUL DID want to erase me from pieces of our future together – not letting me have some say in naming and raising children and dismissing me instead of listening when I told him what I wanted. I wanted more. I wanted it all – the something to feed the hunger, the answer to the mysterious thing I sought. I felt close to finding it all, and I set out to find it with a moral compass destined to break.

12. Narrow River, Wide Sky

I WANTED TO BE EQUAL. MAYBE IF WOMEN WERE SOL-
diers like men, women would be safer. If I were as strong as Paul,
we'd have a right relationship or I'd be free of him.

I went to the post office and signed up for the Selective Service. The clerk laughed, " You're a girl. You don't have to, and they
probably wouldn't take you anyway."

I wanted Mom to know, see me, help me. I didn't know how
to ask.

On the steps, watching the sunset, the fuchsia reds and
golds shifting around the valley, stopping to rest on a tree or a
rooftop or on our shoes and our faces, we didn't have this conversation out loud.

*"You always want me to change. Can't you just love me the way
I am?" I said.*

"But you should change. And I do love you," Mom said.

"But that's not how it feels."

"I'm sure it feels that way, but it isn't that way."

Thinking back and forth between us, combining memory,
intuition, and projection:

"Life is just so hard for heavy girls," she might have said.

"What if I never lose weight?" I did worry.

"Don't talk like that. There's always hope."

"Can't I just be like this?"

We would have sat in the silence.

The light would have turned to purples and dusky browns, sparkling beige, maroon, and charcoal. Fade to black. Scene over.

"You'll lose weight, honey. Don't worry. You just have to try harder, that's all." She said this out loud as she stood up. I'd asked her earlier that day if I could borrow her Richard Simmons book.

Lump in my throat. Lumps in my body stuck to me. My starving soul couldn't shake the feeling that there wasn't enough to nourish me.

After a while, Paul broke up with me every week or so. This lasted a long time. Every time he broke up with me, I found another boy, and there weren't many in that small town.

Larry. We parked Larry's blue Ford Ranch Wagon by the football field along the trees, windows open. I heard the Mancos River, a soft rushing.

Johnny and I went to the drive-n theater in Cortez and had sex in the back of a Chevy four-door.

Ted let me give him a hand job in the living room when no one was home.

Matthew lived in Cortez. I'd had a crush on him in sixth grade and rode my bike back and forth in front of his house so he'd notice me. We sat on the playground in the monster truck tire and held hands for hours. He told me he loved me and kissed me just before he moved to Cortez before seventh grade. We reunited after those years of junior high and high school and had sex in his trailer.

Rick was an insatiable cowboy, twenty-seven years old. A fiddler, Colorado famous.

When Paul and I got back together, he said, "You'd be a terrible wife." So I thought we were done, but like our sex before he graduated from high school, it kept happening.

I wanted some boy to save me. I wanted to save myself.

I kept thinking, *If Joseph Smith could create a new religion because he was a sex maniac, so can I*. I told my brother feminist things – ideas I'd been kicking around, embracing, discarding. I said pornography was against women. He said, "If you were pretty enough, you'd be in porn."

Then something else happened.

Mom said "Never go to parties," and "Parties are dangerous," so I didn't go to parties. It wasn't a party I went to one night. Holly moved to the new apartment building in town – four apartments across the gravel street by the gun and tackle shop (all the streets but two were gravel).

Chris with the almost-monster truck, legal for the road, new to town from Alaska. His father was a rich man.

He said, "I have something to show you upstairs." I went.

And in the span of a moment, I was under him and ashamed and trapped. The edges of memory blur, but I remember some things.

Chris started talking while he was moving in me, and I felt revulsion and the ceiling closed in. Chris talked about Larry, who'd talked about me, about how he had sex with me. I'd had sex with several boys by that point, to get away from Paul, to break out of something, to break rules, to create that new religion. My egalitarian sexual ideals blurry edged and closing in.

I heard the words, "He said your pussy was perfect until it got too wet and loose."

Then he finished.

I got up, no longer held down. Freed. As if I'd never been trapped.

I crossed the gravel to the dirt alley, the weeds growing up between the tire tracks again after the winter's cold and the spring's mud, stepped the two steps at the back door, unlocked.

I paused then and locked the door so when I lay on the bunk – the lower one, the cave, knees curled – I could listen for my brother. Maybe he hadn't taken his key, and I would have to let him in because Mom wasn't home. Neither of us had ever been good with keys.

Nobody ever used the word *pussy* except as a pejorative for weakness. Woman = pussy = weak. I asked Brian to beat up the boy who raped me. He said, "I would, but that guy's really tough."

When I told Mom I didn't want to go to prom with the first boy who asked me, she said, "If you don't, you'll hurt his feelings." I went with him.

Pretty Mike and I went out on a date while Paul went up to the mountains to log for a week.

Pretty Mike said, "I have a rubber."

Blond and blue-eyed, but not in a short and severe Christian haircut kind of way, his jeans had that round mark, the telltale sign of a manly man who chewed tobacco. He smelled like apple shampoo. I'd always loved Pretty Mike. So did all the girls. Since seventh grade, I had wondered what our married life would be like. Now that we were almost graduated and eighteen, we could get married, because in that town people married by twenty-one. Twenty-five was getting too old to marry.

Pretty Mike drove out the dirt road past the gravel road up to Jackson Lake and parked in the trees. I watched the stars in the Milky Way and felt them on my skin in a bright, sweet way for two minutes of bliss, Pretty Mike inside me.

We drove back to town and I smelled like apples. The Pleiades, the Seven Sisters, winked.

Later that night in bed, I worried about Paul finding out because of his temper and even though we were in a breakup phase, he might circle the block in rage, the way he'd started to do when we broke up. When he was in a rage, I'd get that hair-on-the-back-of-the-neck feeling. I'd know. I'd check. There he'd be, pausing at the corner, then at the driveway. Again. Again.

More and more, Paul hated me and I hated him, but we were the children of religion and believed in the fire of hell, and we kept going back to each other for possible redemption through future marriage.

The next day, in school, Mike passed me in the hallway and didn't say a word to me.

I walked down the hall and heard that adolescent laughter,

the knowledge the talk really is about you. Patty said, "Trailer trash." Mike wanted Patty to love him, but she never would because she loved Cowboy Justin.

So she said those two words.

"Trailer trash."

Other girls laughed, too.

Even in that poor town, almost everyone lived in a house.

Mom checked our grammar, told us not to end sentences with prepositions. She made sure we had books in our rooms and told us often that the kids in this town needed more books and fewer things bought with credit cards. She worked as a teacher and as a waitress. Her rules and mixed messages and Shakespeare quotes expressed her desires for our lives.

She didn't raise me to become trailer trash.

My moral compass had spun too far and I was lost.

I waited for lightning to strike me.

I DIDN'T WANT to be good after that.

Mom and I sat on the steps and I cried. She lost her patience and said, "What is wrong with you?"

I told her about how mean Paul had been, about wanting out, about wanting to be safe, and about being ashamed because I couldn't get away from him once and for all. She sighed. I watcher her. Disappointment. Anger. Sorrow. I hadn't wanted to hurt her and hadn't wanted her to be angry with me. She had to go to work at the restaurant.

She said, "I'll support your decision, but we can't tell anyone. I have to work with his mother." I saw that my teenage world and her adult world were shut off from each other and held their own sets of lies and facades.

I broke up with Paul again and again. I'd call him and tell him to stop.

"It's over," I said. I hoped for the last time.

He circled the block. Mom and I watched from the windows. She knew I had to go out from time to time.

There was no police station in Mancos. The county sheriff watched over things, but in that small community, the politics of men didn't serve women – this knowledge we understood but didn't articulate. Besides, what would a sheriff do when I said, "My boyfriend hurts me when we have sex, he forces me to do things I don't want to do, he won't wear a condom, he doesn't want me to be friends with anyone else, he circles the block when we break up, but he never punches me with a closed fist and never leaves a bruise?"

"Be careful," Mom said. "Just be careful."

I worked as a dishwasher at the Silver Peaks Restaurant, lucky to have a winter job. My summer job was food service in the cafeteria by Spruce Tree House at Mesa Verde National Monument. Mom said to know how to type and how to waitress.

I heard a man say to Mom one time, "You're a fine waitress. How come you're not married?"

Mom smiled, wanting to not lose tips. She dreamed of traveling. We dreamed of dinner with dessert instead of one or the other. We dreamed of pants long enough to reach our ankles all school year. We didn't mean to complain.

She said to Brian and me, "I've been to poor places in the world. You don't know what hunger is." We knew better than to talk back.

And I kept my food hiding to myself. It was selfish to want more when she had sacrificed – no new clothes for years for herself, the same automobile since 1972 – for fourteen years. It wasn't suffering, she said, erasing argument and experience. It was hard to argue with "There are so many people who have it far worse" and "I complained that I had no shoes until I met a man who had no feet."

Raised in a childhood of plentiful food, she'd been forced to eat everything on her plate, stuffed beyond her capacity. Now, she didn't have to eat too much. She couldn't imagine our deprivation because hers had been different.

"You have all the choices in the world. You can do anything

you put your mind to," she said, but she didn't understand me well enough to say that.

She and I were different from everyone in town, but that didn't mean we were the same as each other. She had a blind spot when it came to me. She grew up in St. Paul, Minnesota, a big city with multiple high schools, multiple colleges, an international airport. Choices. Decisions. People with all kinds of ideas.

She'd raised me to go to college, too, "A woman has to go to college."

My way paid in full, based on financial need, I got a college acceptance letter to the University of Colorado Boulder. Many people in town told Mom she should have me go closer to home because Boulder could be a shock for a small-town girl like me.

"They don't know," she said. "You're no small-town girl." But she also didn't allow that people were different depending on circumstance. She said, "People are the same wherever you go."

Patty told me that of all the people in town, it shouldn't be me who gets to go to college with taxpayer money.

When I graduated from high school, our grandfather visited from Minnesota and parked in the driveway by the van. The newspaper lady called to ask who was parked there, knowing I was graduating, she wanted to let people know who was in town. Uncle Wils, our rich uncle in Sedona, gave me a boom box – my first. It was the most expensive gift I'd ever received.

Our graduating class had nineteen students. Almost everyone graduated. Five were girls – we were the ones who'd made it without getting pregnant, without needing to take care of family, the ones fortunate enough to finish.

Ed was the valedictorian. He died off the coast of Japan while training for the Navy Seals.

Some people got jobs.

More girls, young women, got pregnant out of wedlock – Kallie, again; Sherri had a daughter. Their children were born victims of small-town gossip. Kallie's son would later die at eighteen after a rock climbing fall. Sherri's daughter would die crossing the road where we went to rent VCRs. She would be twelve.

SOME PEOPLE KEPT going to vo-tech to finish their skillsets.

Ted, who let me give him a hand job, went off to California. He died after running a red light a month after graduation. The head football coach, who wasn't a man given to throwing around compliments, wrote a letter about Ted and his quiet ability to be the underlying strength of the frontline. In the town's tiny newspaper, the coach said that Ted was remarkable in a very unremarkable class.

Huey jumped off the Mancos Hotel, built in 1894 and two stories tall. He broke his arm. His foster family and some other people in town said he was ungrateful for all that had been done for him. He disappeared west of Mancos somewhere.

Patty said I had no common sense. I hated her. I couldn't argue, wanted it not to be true, wanted to point out my common sense versus hers, wanted to defend myself.

Paul and I decided we'd stay together, but he'd date other people. Part of me still believed that if I could change myself that I'd be good enough to change him, and we could become what we were meant to become all along – a loving couple with three children, a doublewide trailer and decent jobs. A happy ending. And yet, I still wanted more.

Ambition. An ugly word, Mom said. It should never be about ambition when I talked to her about my wants. Shame accompanied my dreams.

"You can't date anyone," Paul said, and I said I probably would, but I wouldn't have sex with anyone. I still hadn't thought about birth control. He told me I better not have sex, and he said, "It won't matter if you go to college. You'll still be dumb."

Mancos was changing: the volunteer fire department was updating their emergency system to include pagers, there was now an old folks home, the video store kept getting in new movies and wasn't renting out VCRs as often because people were buying them for themselves with credit cards. New people were moving in who had ideas about llamas and goats and elk ranches. We didn't know it then, but people were about to start paying big bucks to live here.

WHEN MOM DIED and I packed away her belongings, I found letters she'd written but hadn't sent. I read, "Dave, you hurt me in more ways than bruises." I read a repeated line throughout her journals – "Be of Service." I found the journal I'd given her for her birthday. She hadn't written in it yet.

So, I opened it and wrote her a letter.

Mama, how will I live without you? I'm sorry I didn't know more about your life. I'm sorry I told you a story that made you sad. I'm sorry for everything.

"Our memories save us," she'd told me when she gave me a diary for my thirteenth Christmas.

I started writing my memories to save myself from the grief I'd gathered and given, and to figure out how to live without her, to grow up, and to consider what it means to be of service.

IV. You're Not Meant for the Same Things

13. College

MOM SAID, "YOU ALL PACKED?" LOOKING AT MY ROOM, seeing nothing holding me back. She sighed, impatient.

"Yeah."

"So, you're ready."

My throat hurt and the smell of the sage made it hurt more. I'd wanted to leave, but when it came time, I wanted to stay and cry under my crucifix.

Mom turned around, pulling me along with her will. We passed through the trailer: Little scratches in the paneling that triggered memories of games, furniture-moving, fights with my brother, escapes from him. I pet the cats. We'd had many cats over the years. Funny Mike, Paul's best friend, said we lived in a cat house. Now there was Furzy with the big mitten-shaped, extra-toed paws, tall enough to reach the top of the counter in a full stretch, tortoiseshell Thomas, and Fuffy, the cat only six years my junior. Tuxie tilted his head to play when I passed him sitting in the cat window. I knew he'd miss me, but not enough to follow me to Boulder using his cross-Colorado navigation skills. We believed that he'd made his way home from Omaha, Nebraska, where he'd jumped out of the van when we'd gone to visit the Minnesota relatives, taking the cats with us so they wouldn't starve over the summer.

Mom drove me over the mountains, following the highways built in the riverbeds, up to Grand Junction and east on I-70, passing through the valley we'd lived in when Dad lived with us, when we lived with goats and chickens, on the way to the University of Colorado Boulder.

I met my redheaded roommate with the whitest, freckle-dappled skin I'd ever seen, well dressed, and said, "Hello. Where you from?" the first question of importance.

She said, "Beaverton, Oregon – a small town." It sounded small, so I believed her. "Where you from?" she said, looking me up and down. She told me she planned to pledge Alpha Omega something something. I couldn't catch what she said. She looked me up and down again when I said, "What's that mean?"

She said, "You have an accent." I made a mental note to drop the accent that I hadn't been aware of until right at that moment.

She and her best friend sat in the window smoking cloves, talking about a frat party and pledging.

They talked about sisterhood, the sorority houses, the guidance and support, and the future business contact possibilities. My mind opened, excited. Possibilities.

I asked about pledging a sorority, "How can I do that?"

They laughed.

I didn't know anything about sorority girls or Oregon, and I didn't like that she was there on scholarship because her grandmother was one quarter Blackfoot.

I said, "You don't look like an Indian." I didn't believe she needed a scholarship when she didn't even look like an Indian to me, but mostly I didn't believe she needed a scholarship after she'd told me about her big house on fifteen acres and her family's horses.

She said, "It's not up to you to decide if I'm Indian enough."

I had to navigate in different terrain here. Uncharted social terrain. College would open my mind.

I left the room and wandered the halls until I got to the basement filled with rows and rows of chairs and a massive television.

The television of my childhood was a thirteen-inch black and white set. Pretty much everyone had color by then, even in

Mancos, but Mom said, "They all bought theirs on credit, and I don't believe in buying something you can't pay for straight off." We had three channels from Albuquerque.

In the basement, I found my new church and spent many hours worshipping there.

I didn't know what I was doing there in college. Waiting, I guessed. Hoping for direction, support, some magic, and salvation.

I partied. Everyone did – even the wealthy and beautiful and well-adjusted.

Frat party. Big white house, shuttered windows, three floors and a basement. Wood floors. I'd never been in a place like it.

I walked downstairs, drunk, then drunker, or something else. I didn't remember drinking so much.

Colors faded into a pool table, laughter. Humiliation and my head against a wall, then my face on the pool table. Air across my naked backside.

Then nothing.

I heard, "She's so fat" and "Pull up your panties."

My underwear. I pulled them up.

I walked back upstairs, remembering and not remembering. Sober. *How?*

My friends said, "Where have you been?"

"I don't know." They looked at each other in a knowing-glance kind of way.

They walked me out. When I woke up the next morning, I couldn't put together what happened.

I thought, *Why is everyone else doing so well here, and I am falling apart?*

Focus. Plans. Supported by people who had these things. Or they had support in not being focused or support for not having a plan. Support for lack of direction. "Everyone is struggling," said everyone when I reached out to say I needed more help.

I'd been seeking salvation since I'd learned about salvation.

Saving, being saved, saving myself, saving everyone, saving the world. Such beautiful ambition.

The stone steps and the arches and the old trees and the young people walking with purpose from class to class. Wondrous direction.

I wrote letters to Mom. She wrote back saying, "The University of Colorado works hard to make sure everyone succeeds."

I wished I could tell her the truth of things. I wished I could be strong enough to face what I knew she'd say because she always said them: "It's not that bad" and "It could be worse" and "What were you thinking, anyway?"

Still, I hoped.

I wandered. I dabbled. I took French, the only class I attended. I watched the moon over the Flatirons. I missed the stars, which were hidden under city lights.

Then I learned that electricity could be created by pedaling a bicycle, given the proper equipment. I learned that French is not the same as Spanish.

I wanted to be famous for something or change the world or do that big thing that Mom said I could do – anything, she said. I could do anything. I got a radio certification for college radio and played 78s on the 33⅓ setting at midnight.

Brian visited me and I took him to the station. He handed me heavy metal records and we played them until a maintenance worker, a massive Viking descendent, walked in and straight up to me with an evil face. I froze and my heart pounded in my ear, but I could hear Brian say, "Hey, man," and the man turned around and his expression didn't change, but he left. Walked out. Just like that. The man, three times Brian's size in height and weight, left me alone.

We put the records back and left dead air on the radio and ran to the bus stop.

Brian stayed in my college dorm room for a night because my roommate moved out. He left, and I cried – grateful to have a brother.

Even though my Pell Grant covered all of my expenses, I got a job in a nursing home. I felt a terrible guilt for needing and receiving when so many people needed but didn't receive. "You're uppity," Patty said. "You think you're better than everybody else," Paul told me I thought I was too good for Mancos and too good for him.

As a nurse's aide, I forced the elderly out of bed in the mornings and forced them back in at night. Forced them to eat, tied them into their beds and chairs so they wouldn't fall. It was in the name of safety, but safety to what end? After my full eight-hour shifts, after forty-hour weeks, my guilt and I went out drinking and dancing.

I got another roommate – Lynn, from Chicago. She and I went out dancing at the bars frequented by black college kids, "To be with other black people," she said. She said I was okay to go with her if I didn't say anything awful – "White people want to be like us until it comes to actually being black. Don't try to be us. Just be yourself," she said.

I invited her to go home with me during the break from school, but she wouldn't. She said, "Are there any black people there?" and "I know your town, and I'm not going there." I said I'd protect her, but she laughed.

I skipped most of my classes except French and ecology.

I dated other boys the way I told Paul I would, and I did have sex with them. There was the blond boy with a name I don't remember, who I met at a frat party, and Anthony, the CU Buffalo's fullback, and Afshin from Iran, who studied nuclear physics, and Eric, whose family friends were the Coors family, and Matt with the trust fund – what a concept. Not one of them chewed tobacco.

I failed all my finals, except French, and got a letter that said my financial aid would be taken away if I didn't bring my GPA up.

During the Christmas break, I went back across the divide on a Greyhound bus and went out with Paul a few hours after getting back into town.

I woke up one night, a few days later, knowing something had happened.

I looked outside and saw Paul parked by the tree at the end of the driveway, his white truck lit by a full moon.

Then I walked into the living room and I huddled by my sleeping mother.

"So tired," she rolled away from me.

I walked to the trees at the end of the long driveway and got into the truck.

Paul drove south on Main out into the spaces where small ranchers sold out and became homeowners with acreage. A few cows, not too many. The cows were north mostly. We drove south toward the reservation.

He stopped the truck at the border of a dirt road and then said, "You sure are fat."

"Yeah. Sorry."

"Why don't you lose weight? You're such a pig."

"I'm getting out now."

"Why did you get in the truck with me?" he said. "You got me all worked up, like we're gonna get back together, and now you're gonna leave? You're such a bitch."

My face turned hot and I glowed sweat and ugliness, I looked to the stars for comfort, but they blurred.

He picked a boot off the floor, a work boot, and threw it, and it hit the mirror, then landed back on the floor where it had been. He could've hit me, but he controlled himself, threw it instead, without a target. His rear-view mirror broke off. And then he got mad.

Ever aware of door handles, escape routes, I jumped out of the truck into the cold night and walked along the gravel, wishing I'd worn my tennis shoes instead of leather clogs.

He drove up behind me.

"Get in."

"No."

"You can't walk all the way back to town."

"Why?"

"You're such a baby. Get in. I'm not gonna hurt you."

"I'm pregnant."

The world stopped, but I walked. The truck inched forward.

"You have to get in."

"Did you hear me?" I turned into him, looked straight through the open truck window, straight into his eyes.

"I promise I won't hurt you. Just get in. You can't walk all the way back to town."

It was cold. I got in. I was always getting into that truck. He cut the engine when I got in. Country boy power play.

"I'll marry you," he said.

"That won't work out," I said.

"Are you sure it's mine?" he said.

"I'm sure. Pretty sure," I said. I thought it happened the night we were parked out north of Hesperus on a gravel road. He didn't pull out in time. I felt it or heard it – a whispered spark. The next morning I knew that I was pregnant.

But then in that moment when he asked if I was sure that it was his, I knew something truer – I'd slept with other men. I didn't know that this baby was his for sure.

"You're right," I said. "It might not be yours."

Wind, cows lowing, leaves rattling. Darkness and the moon's lightness. The smell of cooking oil in far-off pots, burn barrels and smoke, frogs and crickets and coyotes. But I still felt alone – the only woman who'd ever been pregnant.

He said, "What are you gonna do?"

"I don't know," I said. "But I want to go home now."

He started up the truck, dropped me off at the end of the long driveway, and never circled the block again.

As we walked to church, Mom said, "I think my mother died of cancer caused by her grief over living with my father." She stopped to pet Posie, our cat who waited beside the gravel road across from church for us and had stepped into our path for a pet.

Mom stood and held my soft hand with her calloused one, again, as we walked, "Such a tyrant."

The callouses reminded me of Jesus' wounds. I wanted to be healed and choked down my sob and watched clouds drift along – clouds, such a comfort.

I couldn't help thinking about the injustices – my grandmother's cancer and my grandfather's tyranny and about my everything. I wanted to argue with Mom about grief causing cancer and the injustice in holding a person responsible for their own cancer, about how women have fewer choices than men, about feminism and science, but Mom, for all her independence and reason and wisdom, wouldn't have heard a word. She'd have heard me arguing and contradicting.

We walked along – soft skin and callouses.

I sat in church, thinking about the many seasons of flower arrangements, paired with particular curtain colors, symbols matching symbols, something comforting, but constraining about the order of it all and listening to Father Rising talk about forgiveness.

"How does a person forgive the unforgiveable?" he asked. "If we forgive our oppressors, we are both freed. If Jesus could forgive his torturers, then surely we can forgive anyone the grievances of our daily lives and the larger hurts in human relationships."

Father Rising wore his humble clothes that day instead of the gold-embroidered robe, tasseled and silk-threaded.

I looked up at the stained glass, seeking a way to forgive, hearing freedom in Father Rising's words. The stained glass window shown yellows and browns, greens and reds near the organ where Mom sat waiting for her cues. Saint Paul is lying on the ground and a light shines on him as he looks up at the words, "Saul, Saul, why persecutest thou me?"

My grandmother's face half smiled down at me, her skin, a dapple of colors – an impression in stained glass. If someone else had looked over just then they might not have been able to make her out, but it was her.

She said, "Your grandfather took my whole life. I had options, you know, having been quite intelligent, but then I got sick, and he took care of me."

Father Rising's wife never smiled.

I sat there and thought, *Of course they want us to forgive.*

Mom turned back in her pew and smiled, then looked sad and turned away so fast, unsure I'd seen it.

I looked back at the stained glass, my grandmother gone.

So that day I decided forgiveness belonged to priests, to men, and to Jesus.

No justice in forgiveness exists, I thought. My faith in God was done.

I went back to Boulder after the Christmas break.

Boulder's Flatirons had been a symbol of victory a few months before, but now, failing in college and on academic probation, I couldn't muster the energy to get to classes, but I had to get out of the dorm to end the pregnancy.

None of the people walking in the world, on the sidewalks and through the university campus, no one knew I was pregnant. Boulder wasn't a small town like Mancos – many more people, stories, liberals, many more people who weren't white or Christian. I never saw anyone with a gun rack. I felt safer there in the city, but still lonely – I hadn't counted on that. There were more people who didn't know each other or care for each other. They didn't need each other. They got along without help as long as they had money.

The bus dropped me off in front of a two-story office building.

I waited in the front room until the nurse called me back.

She asked the personal questions.

I didn't cry. I thought I deserved the humiliation.

The receptionist said, "Where's Mancos?" When I told her southwest Colorado, between Durango and Cortez, she said, "Oh, that's such a beautiful area. Lucky you."

"Do you want to hold my hand?" the nurse said. "This is going to be very painful." She wore a thick tennis bracelet with many rows of jewels. I worried the bracelet would pinch me when she extended her hand.

"Okay," I said, so afraid. I willed myself to think of her hand as someone else's hand. I couldn't think of whose.

It hurt. When I'd gone to CU's health services, I got the name of the abortion provider and the cost. No insurance was offered. I wouldn't have known to ask. I couldn't afford the fee it would cost to be put under. Two hundred dollars for the procedure and five hundred with anesthesia. I didn't have the three hundred more dollars. God got in one last punch as my faith drained away.

Lynn took care of me. She'd had to come get me because I'd forgotten underwear and had no way to get home.

"Why didn't you wear underwear?" she laughed and sympathized, shook her head and hugged me. She wasn't a hugger, so I cried harder.

I cried from the cramps and bled more than I'd ever bled.

Later that evening, Lynn said, "I'll just have the baby if I get pregnant. I don't want to go through what you're going through."

"I bet having a baby hurts a whole lot more than this," I said.

"No way," she said. Then she said, "And even if it does, you're hurting in other ways, too."

"Yeah, but I know it wouldn't be okay for me to have a baby now."

She nodded.

I called Paul that night from the basement where the mailboxes sat. The cold tile hurt my feet. I didn't think I deserved to wear socks.

I told him the abortion was done.

He said, "So."

I said, "I thought you'd want to know."

"You said it might not be mine," he said. "And we're not together."

"Yeah. It's not on you. It's on me." He was Catholic. I'd fallen from my religion, no hope left for my soul.

I told him it hurt, that I couldn't afford the anesthesia.

"You brought it on yourself," he said. I got angry, "You will never feel this kind of pain," I yelled, "because you're a man. You think things are equal. I can't shoot deer or people, and you can't have an abortion, but that's – "

He hung up before I could finish.

I went back upstairs. My roommate played *Purple Rain* for me over and over.

I was free.

14. Boys Who Didn't Chew Tobacco

I SAW A PINK FLOYD LASER LIGHT SHOW IN DENVER with a Mancos boy, two years older, a junior at CU. Pat's parents had been professors and worked at Mesa Verde National Park, where they lived, about ten miles from the town where I grew up. Of all the boys I had sex with in Mancos, besides Paul, Pat was the one I wanted to love me, but he loved Wendy, who had a perfect face and matching grace, money and a good reputation. A Mormon.

Because they were scientists, educated, etc., they'd never really been trapped in Mancos the way some people were, the way I thought I'd been or wanted to be so that I could have that sunset every night, the one that saved me whether or not I believed in God.

I believed I could settle into my schoolwork if I knew what would happen to me, if I could just know how it would all turn out.

Other college girls were beautiful, charming, funny, sweet, smart, a million great things – not all of them, but some impossible combination. I had big breasts and blond hair and a forty-hour work week at a nursing home, where I had to rush to clean bedpans and worse and didn't have time to listen to them cry.

Instead of taking the gift of education, I worked at the nursing home and partied and went out dancing.

I slept with boys who didn't chew tobacco and had never fired a gun.

I went to bars and looked for a husband to save me.

I saw him one night, my savior, sitting there at the back of the bar in a room off the side of the main space, backlit by a bright orb of light that shone on the dance floor. Several beautiful women sat at the table with him at the head, his hands clasped and resting in front of him.

In that moment, I was drunk and formerly deeply religious. My friends said, "Where you going?"

I didn't say a word, just pushed aside their blockade of hands to the promised land of my savior.

Do you think I'm beautiful? Do you want to make me a good woman again and marry me? The children will be beautiful, can't you see?

By grace, I didn't say these things, but my body language did. The women parted the way.

Then I sat down and straightened my posture and pushed out my boobs toward him

His eyes widened and hope grew in me, and then he said, "Yes. I see them."

And he didn't say anything else.

I felt almost sober with humiliation, and he no longer appeared to me as Jesus.

I slid down the seat and to the bathroom.

Boulder was Hari Krishnas speaking magic words for you, and everyone was a stranger and some wanted to be strange. Boulder was partying and college kids and people making money off college kids and partying. Boulder was knowledge and spiritual awakenings for sale. It was Flatirons and cold wind and many buildings and transient society, many roads everywhere. Access to everything. Boulder was hippies and happiness and too many choices for a small-town girl accustomed to wanting more. Boulder was lost in excess.

I left my job at the nursing home after something terrible happened. One of the employees, a nurse's aide drew in marker all over a woman's body. Disturbing messages, evil graffiti. The woman couldn't speak. She'd been traumatized. I'd been working the wing she lived on, so it was my responsibility in a way because, How did it happen while I worked in the other patients' rooms, they said. While they didn't think I had a part in it, they didn't tell me it wasn't my fault either. They didn't want me to leave unless I wanted to after a two-hour questioning that left me more confused than assured. *Who'd do something like that? What had he done exactly?* They didn't tell me the specifics, or if they did I couldn't grasp them. I left because I was afraid of the lack of security – so many ways into the nursing home, so many windows and doors. I left even knowing I'd need the money because I'd be losing my Pell Grant.

For my birthday, I went to the doctor because I felt so tired all the time – mononucleosis.

"Do your own thang," the poster said, decorated with flowers and sunshine – curving strips of friendly orange and yellow fire. It lay on top of my empty dorm room desk, everything packed, ready for Mom to pick me up in the van and drive me back to Mancos. My gut turned with the humiliation of it.

I'd had opinions about everything. I wanted to change the world with words – I thought about journalism, but I hadn't been going to class.

None of the boys I'd had sex with came to say goodbye. I knew they wouldn't, but I'd hoped. Beautiful, tall, strong Barry brought a little box of See's chocolates, and I'd never slept with him. He whispered in my ear, "Are you okay?" and I said, "No, but yeah," and he said, "Because you know last night when you were drunk, you said some things about killing yourself because nothing really matters." I said, "It's from working in the nursing home is all. The end of life is horrible, and I'm worried that it's all just living in a house and having a family and then just having that be the end." He nodded and said to take care and he kissed me on the cheek. He kissed me freely, as a gift.

I'd always been a real talker, but that day I cried and had nothing to say.

"You need to find another way around," said Lynn, my chemical engineering roommate, on her way to Chicago after graduation from CU. Chicago would put her back together, she said, "I can be black again."

She said, "You're not meant for the same things. You have other, um, skills."

We all laughed – the other two girls who were also successful – one a biology major and the other an artist who said she'd be an architect and do other art on the side. I had no doubt they'd all do what they said they'd do.

My skills weren't marketable. My opinions weren't worth much because I didn't know how to articulate them.

"What will I do?" I said.

Lynn pointed at the poster, then she said, "Your own thang," a gift, I knew – her allowing that bit of her culture through for me. She protected herself, rightly, from my ignorance and told me I could never mimic her. "Don't copy me if you can't be me," she'd say.

"You all are so smart," I said.

"It isn't that you're not smart," Lynn said. We all laughed again. Then she said, "You have other things to do right now."

Mom and I drove over the mountains and across the Continental Divide, the van filled with memory: goats and dirt roads, sage, and ponderosas, and rivers, the canoe strapped to the top, Fuffy's cat crate rattling around. The frozen plastic water bottle sat melting between us, as ever. When Mom drank, she gulped harder than usual. She hissed and avoided my eyes and gulped, the ice thudding around across the miles.

The wide blue sky shed too much light on me, on my failure.

I thought I'd be transformed from a big fish in a little pond to a little fish in a bigger pond filled with bright schools of fish where I'd be safer from predators in the mass. Instead, I'd done myself in – allowed myself to be swallowed by viruses and fear, alcohol and indecision.

I transformed, but not in the way I'd hoped.

Mom kept both hands on the wheel, white knuckles, finger-nails scraping against each other in small flicks of fury I could feel, drumbeats in my chest, as she watched the scenery and the road winding. I saw that she saw bighorn sheep and eagles, but this time she didn't point them out. She shook her head from time to time and sighed and clicked her tongue. And she whispered and hissed. In those few short months at CU, I'd forgotten about that whispering.

That hissing.

I used to ask her, "Are you mad at me?"

And she'd say no.

That day, I knew I'd caused the serpentine cursing.

I watched the small whitewater rivers, the winding streams, and the hemmed-in irrigated ditches, and wished I could stop and listen. I wished I hadn't tried to swim into an ocean of a big pond – a small-town girl at the biggest party school in the western United States.

I went back to my room at the end of the trailer and slept and slept. From time to time, I got out of bed and sat by the river, lined with birch, maple, and pine and watched the movement of water around rocks. I listened to all the small waves and crashes and turned stones over and over in my hands.

There were times I suffered abdominal pain and couldn't do anything but get through it. I'd suffered it most of my life. We called it "Nerves" and waited it out.

I lay in bed for months by the open window – first lavender, then sage, then the dry grass of summer, and so many rainstorms marked the passing of time – until Mom said, "Get up now. Get a job."

I worked in the nursing home in Cortez. Vern let me use his truck, and Mom let me use her car. I walked with mud heavy on my shoes for many more months after that, but I kept a job, kept doing what people do.

One day coming home from work, I hit a deer – an older fawn. I hadn't been speeding. I saw a hind end of a fawn, hit the brakes too late, another fawn leaped in front, fleeing, but I ran her down, my foot on the brake. I pulled over and hugged her, she made a terrible sound and fell heavy from my arms. I turned to see her mother heading away, the other fawn close to her haunches disappearing into a dust cloud hanging in the air. An off-duty police officer stopped and put me back together so I could drive home. "No damage to the car," he said. He pulled the baby far off the shoulder for the coyotes. I smelled the wild scent of deer and blood and fresh death on my clothes all the way home.

I went to Brian's room seeking comfort. He said, "You have to be an idiot to hit a deer."

MOM AND I sat on the steps like we'd done many times, but I didn't tell her about the deer – she'd be so angry. We watched the sunset turn the La Plata Mountains to lavender and the western sage to fuchsia, blood red through the clouds until the blackness of night. I clenched my teeth and tasted blood.

Mom said Dad clenched his teeth, too. Everything he did disgusted her. She once spanked me for biting my nails like he did. I vowed to be anything but him. Dad had gone to Brian's high school graduation but not mine.

I regretted signing up for Selective Service. I changed my mind about women being more like men and wanted men to be more like women.

At some point, Mom sighed and said, "Sometimes, it takes a long time to leave." I thought she meant how long it took me to leave Paul.

"But I don't love him," I said, "And I'm glad he's left me alone now."

"Took me a long time to leave your father," she said, "but I'm not necessarily talking about them."

She got up and went back inside, the screen door twanged.

I went out with a man from the Cortez branch of our church – we'd met during our teen years at church functions. It wasn't that I wanted to go back to church, but he seemed safe – familiar. He had a round baby face and freckles and drove a big truck.

After a couple of months, Shawn and I sat on his bed in his parent's house, and I handed him a box with a blue bow on it. He wore cowboy clothes with sharp, red western piping.

When Shawn saw the box, he started shaking his head.

I smiled and said, "Open it."

The salesman had tried to talk me out of it, "Who's this for?"

"Um, a boy."

"Hmm," he said. "You can't get your money back. This is the Toggery, not some thrift store." He looked me up and down.

"I know," I said as if I knew.

When Shawn opened the box, he said, "You have to take it back."

I told him that the guy at the store said I couldn't.

"You shouldn't have bought it for me, then."

The watch had a cowboy engraving – a cowboy on horseback roping a longhorn in the middle of a storm. There was so much captured there on that watch cover – something I though Shawn would want, and if I gave it to him, he'd understand something and love me.

Shawn asked me why I bought a watch for him. I tried to tell him, but then I said, "Because I love you."

He said, "Well, I don't love you, and I won't ever love you. I don't want to go out with you anymore."

I'm sure I cried. I'm a crier.

I'd run out of birth control pills and used sponges. Shawn used condoms, one of the few men who did when they had sex with me.

I dated other men.

One day, Mom said, "Do you have something to tell me?"

She held the jar I had not-so-thoughtfully hidden on top of the back of the toilet. She held it in front of her as if holding something fragile – precious.

She said, "Usually when someone has a jar on the toilet it means they're taking a urine sample for a pregnancy test."

Trapped, I sunk to the floor and said, "Mom, I'm going to

hell." I cried into my hands. Defeated. Vulnerable. Whatever she would say, I'd take.

But she didn't judge or chide. She softened into a mother I hadn't seen before, the one I'd wanted all along – the one I needed all along. She kneeled on the floor with me.

She said, "I'll support you if you want to get an abortion. I'll support whatever you decide."

I told her I already had an abortion, so this would be a second one.

She said, "Well, I have something to tell you, too, but you have to keep my secrets to the grave."

She and I were hell-bound together. We sat on the floor and cried and laughed. Secrets we held rushed to the surface.

She took me to Durango to the closest Planned Parenthood. I wasn't pregnant then, just late. We talked about birth control. We didn't talk about sin ever again.

That moment was the beginning of confessions between us. Our confessions in church directed us along a particular and familiar moral compass, but our confessions to each other freed us. I became adept at finding the right place and time for speaking difficult truths, but Mom struggled. She'd had more practice keeping secrets. Her confessions were random and sudden, urgent.

One day, she said, "You know, I was pregnant with you before I got married."

I didn't know. We were shopping at the mall in Durango, a new formation in the landscape, when she said this. I pushed shirts around on the rack, looking at them, looking at her.

"Abortion was illegal then," she said.

I kept my balance. I thought of Patty pushing me down and me getting back up. I said, "Can we go sit down?"

We sat under a fake mall tree. Mom bought ice cream. She ate rocky road. I ate praline pecan.

I TOLD MOM about the babysitter who'd kept me in the Benway's bathroom when I was a child.

Mom said, "Oh, that poor thing. I wonder what happened to her to make her that way." Mom raised me to think of others first, mostly a beautiful ideal, but not in that moment, not regarding that time when I was five and the babysitter was sixteen.

I said, "That's not cool, Mom."

She said, "What?"

"Worrying about her and not me," I said.

"Oh, well, of course, you're fine," she said.

Even though I felt hurt that she'd said what she said, I knew she was right. I was fine. I'd be fine.

And the worst was over.

15. What'll You Be When You Grow Up?

I WOKE UP TO MOM STANDING AT THE EDGE OF THE BUNK crying.

She said, "My father died. I was going to visit him in two weeks." She held an envelope in her hand, turning it over and over – the plane ticket.

I held her.

She said, "Just two weeks."

When she recovered some, she said, "I guess they'll sell the farm, too."

She was thinking of those forty acres that became twenty in St. Paul. Those acres would grow houses and apartment buildings and never grow anything else. I thought about what would be erased – the apple orchard and the deer, even as resilient as they are. I remember running through the fog among the trees and winding my way through the raspberries, skin cut and snagged by thorns, and the taste of sweet summer and the place where, we believed, my mother's mother's ghost came to rest.

Grandpa was soap and dry-clean scent and warm hands, brown spotted with age. Born on May Day, 1900, he never complained except about people – most didn't work hard enough or discipline their children well enough or didn't have enough faith in the divine. He quoted Benjamin Franklin.

He said to me, "You walk this way, but you should walk this way" – something about my knees bending at the wrong moment in my stride.

To Mom, he said, "Don't you think Brian is shy and overactive?"

He wore his usual suit and tie, the way of his generation.

When he tended the orchard in Minnesota, he changed into beige work clothes.

After the news of his death, Mom and I sat on the steps watching another southwest Colorado sunset. She said, "Everything just changed."

Over the next year, we made the small changes that became everything.

WHILE I'D BEEN away, Brian had had his own life, listening to heavy metal – Queensrÿche and Scorpions and Black Sabbath and figuring out what to do next. He bought a muscle car, a Mercury Comet, for a few hundred dollars with money he'd saved, and then totaled it because the steering wheel came loose, close to where the river runs under the road up to the cemetery. Mom told me she'd warned him the car barely ran and was too good to be true.

Brian didn't like school. He didn't have a father to help in business – logging or working on a ranch or doing construction. He could work in a mine – gypsum, molybdenum, coal, or vanadium. He'd have to migrate for work or work seasonally, like so many small-town boys.

An army recruiter sat at our kitchen table and told Brian to sign his life away with a laugh. Just like that. The recruiter hadn't been allowed on the high school property, yet half the boys in my brother's class had the same conversation and signed the same papers at their own family tables.

When the army recruiter told my brother to sign, I said, "Mama, if mothers would not let their sons fight, there would be no more war."

She stood against the wall drying her hands with the dishtowel and said, "If you can stop him, go ahead and try."

Brian said he could still be a writer. He wrote stories about wolves and ranchers and wilderness. He still read his stories to me in the middle of the night.

"Wake up, Jenny, I have a good one. Tell me how it sounds," he said that night after he'd signed the papers and there was no going back to how things had been when we played in the trees and scrambled up stone mountains and into cliff overhangs and wandered the high sage and piñon pine desert and the rocky, cold mountains, when he dreamed of finding a gold mine, and I dreamed of moving away and becoming famous.

He read about wolves and I listened, happy to be forgiven for having cried when he signed the papers for the army.

He went to basic training, and when I saw him next he had muscles, even in his neck. "They take out who you are and put a soldier in his place," Brian said.

When we first moved to Mancos, Mom saved the great horned owl, and he sometimes got stuck under Brians's bed, shaking it with his wing flapping.

Brian would scream in the night, "Mom. The owl's under my bed. Hurry!"

He'd tell the story later that Hootie seemed like a ghost under his bed, hooting and trapped.

And then even later, Brian talked about blanket parties during basic training, where everybody puts a bar of soap in a pillow case and pounds on the guy deemed to have deserved it. The blanket party.

Brian had to participate.

"If you don't join in, they'll do it to you next."

MOM FOUND A teaching job in Denver making three times what she'd made in Mancos, and she moved there. "Just goes to show what unions can do," she said.

She lived and worked for several years in Denver.

THE ARMY STATIONED Brian in Germany, and he wrote to tell us about his German girlfriend from Saarbrücken and his tattoo of a black eagle. His girlfriend sent me a pair of earrings she'd made of soft metal.

I lived in employee housing up at Mesa Verde National Monument, not far from Mancos, in a doublewide trailer, where I shared a bedroom with one of the janitorial staff, who never spoke to me. The trailer was five bedrooms on either side of a narrow hallway, two people per room. The twenty of us shared one bathroom – one toilet, one shower. I worked at the Far View Lodge bussing tables and waitressing in the noisy restaurant overlooking hundreds of miles of juniper and piñon and the volcanic formations of southern Colorado and New Mexico.

Then I found Joe. He worked as a waiter.

We had a coworker who could whistle like a bull elk, and he fooled me every time. I'd run to the window to see.

Alonzo always laughed about it and would say, "What're you lookin' for?"

I didn't know, but Joe asked if I wanted to live with him in Phoenix.

I carried my last tray of dishes with leftover "Anasazi bread" and corn salsa and rabbit meat to the kitchen and packed my clothes into my backpack and got the shuttle down to Cortez, then rode the Greyhound to Denver to see Mom, and then I decided.

I told her, "I'm going to Phoenix – the big city, at last. When people ask me why I'm going, I'll tell them I'm going to school there. I won't tell them there's a boy there, and I'm going to live with him. And I won't tell them I don't know whether I'm going to travel agent school or to technical school. I'm still deciding on that."

Mom bought my plane ticket. She put unsalted sunflower seeds in a baggie for the flight.

At the airport, waiting at the gate, we held hands.

We hugged each other for a long time. She said, "You better go."

I didn't want to. "I think I'm leaving Colorado forever."

She nodded. We felt the truth of it. The depth of it. It wasn't New York City or Hollywood, but it was a city. City enough.

On the plane, I watched through tears as the mountains gave way to brown and red earth canyons and saguaro and barrel cactus. Phoenix, I told myself, would be my place now. I'd learn to manage this thirst I had for more. In Phoenix, I couldn't believe the golf courses and fountains and palm trees. In January of my twenty-first year, Joe and I moved in with his friend Fred for a week until we found an apartment. They lived in a suburb in a light beige house at the end of a cul-de-sac. His wife, Gigi, was expecting twins and didn't seem happy about us being there, but she was the best kind of good woman for the kind of man Fred was, the kind who seeks loyalty and compliance but calls it partnership and equality. Fred sold used cars. He wanted his wife to work because he did. It wasn't fair, he said, if he had to work and she didn't. When the twins were born, Gigi did everything (housework and paid work) after she took a few days off after a caesarian to deliver her daughters. Fred said she was lucky not to have to push babies out "like the women in the fields" and "in the old days." He celebrated that her vagina wasn't stretched by birth. He and Joe high-fived over that.

Joe's brother-in-law lived in Phoenix and let me use his Datsun B-210, yellow with purple-tinted windows and a blue stripe. I loved that car.

I worked at a domestic violence shelter as a receptionist. The intake building was next door, loud and dramatic. I wasn't allowed there because I didn't have training.

"And God only knows what you'll say to people," a counselor said. The head counselor, Sarah, gave me pages of intake forms to retype because the old copies were becoming illegible, she said. There were sentence starters, "1. When I was a little child, my father..." and "2. My mother always worried about..." and "3. What I really want is..." "4. ... "

In my mind, I answered the questions as the touch-type electric typewriter tapped along ninety words per minute:

… called me a little shit when I broke the closet door – because he wasn't fast enough to catch me to spank me. I'd outrun him again.

… money and what other people thought.

… to be right, to be good, to be loved, to change the world, to get myself together.

Joe and I didn't get along well. He told me I couldn't cook or clean and that I needed to make more money. He said, "You're always complaining about how I treat you."

In February, just after my twenty-first birthday, Joe got mad and punched a hole in the wall. I called Mom, afraid. I thought she'd be angry – I hadn't trusted her transformation as the understanding mother she'd become since the day she discovered the jar on the toilet, the day she'd learned I'd had an abortion in college, the day she'd shared her own secrets. I didn't think she could help anyway. But she drove to Phoenix and gave me the car – a green Honda Accord she inherited from her father. She found a studio apartment for $300 and paid my rent – it was almost four times more than the rent for the trailer we'd lived in, but now she could afford it plus her own rent. She said she wouldn't do it for long.

Mom said, "I know it'll take time to break up with Joe."

I felt guilty, but still battling loneliness, I kept seeing him. I chose Joe over loneliness time and again the way I'd chosen Paul over being alone. But I was also afraid. When we were moving my stuff into the apartment, I rushed Mom into the apartment and said, "Hurry, close the door."

She said, "You stop this. What is wrong with you?"

"I don't want people to see that I live here alone, Mom."

She tsk'd and hissed. She whispered.

"Nobody's watching," she said.

I tried to believe her, tried to relax. I was afraid of Paul finding me. I was afraid of strangers – I walked quick and close to the wall up to my apartment, kept the curtains drawn.

"You'll be fine," she said and went back to Denver.

I made a list of advantages and disadvantages to choose

between travel agent school and technical school. I decided to go to DeVry Institute of Technology. The ratio of men to women was about twenty to one, and the loan office window sat right next to the admissions office window. Class times were scheduled during early evening so more people could keep jobs during daytime hours.

I was sitting on the steps in the bright Arizona sun near the end of March when a tall blond man walked up to me. I could see that he wanted to talk. He was holding a large, fast food drink cup.

He said hello, and I asked him what he was drinking. When he told me, I asked for a drink of his Diet Pepsi.

He said, "I'm Ron. You're so pretty," the magic words.

He said he believed in love at first sight.

When he asked if I'd like to go to Dairy Queen, I said yes.

I kept seeing Joe, too, for a while.

After class in the middle of July, Ron walked me to my car and said, "Don't you wear a seat belt?"

"Do you think I'm going to get in an accident – that I'm a bad driver?" I flipped my keys in and out of my palm.

He tilted his head, confused, as we stood in the hot Phoenix sun, the hairspray in my hair melting. He said he wanted me to be safe, that telling a person to be safe was how he showed he cared. "Do it for me," he said. I did. I thought about the words in my mind when I cringed at his concern – I wondered why his worry felt like an indignity. He made me think about many things because his life had been different – more middle class, he'd lived in a house his mother and step-father paid a mortgage on, his step-father replaced his father soon after the divorce, he had a computer at home, he'd gone to concerts throughout his teen years and spent his free time in malls.

Ron had had a full-time job since he was eighteen – assembly-line work, making parts for electronic scales.

He said, "There was a cleaning unit they told us never to put our hands in because of some super high ultrasonic thing that would eat your flesh off. I was pretty terrified during that whole thing, but Vic took a chance hiring me with no experience. I told them to give me two weeks, and if I didn't perform, they didn't have to pay me."

I'd call him at work, where someone would retrieve him. I'd call his apartment, and he'd answer. I fell in love with his stability, his reliability, his solid-oak soul.

Because Mom had money now – the inheritance from the sale of her father's farm, she went on vacations and didn't need a second job to do it, and she took me with her a couple of times.

We went to Cozumel and went scuba diving in the coral and white sand and bright fish sea.

She took me to Europe, and we visited Brian in Baumholder, Germany, where he was stationed. We went sightseeing during the rainy season in a land of deep green foliage and castles and thick walls of long-populated cities and wide slow rivers and people using trains instead of cars.

Brian and I decided we could tell the Americans from their gait – a long, confident stride, we said. Brian had an even thicker neck and his hair was longer than the basic training buzz but had to be kept short above his ears. Even though my brother is not a tall man, he carries himself big.

And he said, "Have you noticed that nobody speaks to you in anything but English?"

Mom nodded.

"People see that you're American," Mom said, "Americans are fat."

I pulled my shirt away from my belly, trying for a baggy disguise.

Brian said, "It's something else, though."

They looked at each other in that silent way they always had. "Something else," they agreed. It wasn't good, whatever it was.

We left Brian after a few days of visiting. He went back to the base.

Mom and I signed up for language classes in Spain – Mom in the advanced class. I was down the hall in a roomful of Europeans, where mostly we spoke in English and talked about politics and world events.

A German man said, "Let's hear from the young American. Do you think Americans should do anything they wish to do?"

The Europeans laughed when I said, "You can do anything you put your mind to."

I'd misunderstood the question, I gathered, from the confused looks. Eyebrows lifted, heads shaking.

The German man said, "Americans are sort of sweet."

Everyone laughed.

He said, "I was speaking to a larger political agenda."

A woman from the Netherlands said, "Wait. Do you really believe you can do anything you put your mind to?"

"I do," I said. "You could even become president if you work hard enough."

They laughed louder, continued to shake their heads. "Does that apply to everyone in the world – that everyone everywhere just has to work hard enough?" said the French woman.

I sat in silence – stunned. Stumped.

"Americans," the German man repeated, yelling it, looking at the ceiling, hands in the air as if begging God.

The conversation opened up to criticize America in more ways.

"Have you noticed how on their televisions shows they will sleep with everyone, but they won't smoke cigarettes," the teacher said. More laughter.

"Naïve," said the French woman.

"Aren't you afraid there?" a man from Portugal said.

"Well…" I couldn't answer. I wasn't supposed to be afraid. I thought about guns and gun racks and cowboys and history and men and how I closed the door quickly behind me and kept the curtains drawn. Was I afraid in the way he meant?

The room seemed full of shaking heads.

Mom and I stepped off a catamaran onto the north coast of Africa in Tangier.

Very thin women, dressed in light, flowing dresses, many with head coverings, walking through with children, not stopping, while men in white, some also with head coverings, gathered in groups in the square – no jeans, no circular rings on back pockets, no trucks with loaded gun racks, no deer with hanging tongues draped over tailgates.

A man with a basket swayed while a cobra hissed at him.

An old woman, made of bones and skin, carried a heavy basket and cried as she walked along. Children asked us for money, offered to take us places, to find things for us. They patted their bellies, signaling hunger.

Some things seemed staged – mostly it was a tourist town, but unlike any I'd imagined or seen.

I thought I'd seen poverty – so much hunger, violence, and agony in those mountain towns.

But this was different.

Mom said, "Good. I'm glad you're seeing what I want you to see." She'd come from the city where her family had twenty acres with horses; she'd worn hoop skirts and poodle skirts and gone to a school big enough to have a choir and a church big enough to skip a service or two without everyone knowing or even minding. Then she raised us in a trailer and cried when we asked for lunch money. I felt anger at her for saying this to me.

As if … as if …

"Sure, Mom," I said, because it wasn't as if she were wrong either.

A man with nystagmus, his eyes oscillating, bent in a make-shift wheelchair he had to operate with one crooked arm, sat at an uncomfortable-looking angle. Everything on him looked pained – bent limbs with bent feet and hands and bent digits. And there were burn scars.

The tour guide said, "Parents maim their children to make tourists more sympathetic to their begging. It's best to ignore these people."

Mom looked at me, then back at the man and his wheelchair,

then at the tour guide, and emptied her purse into the basket attached to the wheelchair.

We didn't have bus money when we got back to the other side of the Mediterranean, dolphins alongside the catamaran, and me suffering seasickness right there by the Rock of Gibraltar.

I thought about Ron on the flight back across the Atlantic Ocean.

Mom visited Phoenix and picked me up at DeVry.

"You got a VCR," she said, as I got into the car and before I even shut the door.

"VCR? Yeah."

She whispers and hisses. "I paid your rent and gave you grandpa's car, and you got a VCR."

Then I realized she thought I bought it.

"No. No. No. It's Ron's. He's letting me borrow it."

"Sure," she said.

My skin burned, heart raced, I started talking, "It's true. He has more than me. He has everything. He buys things like that. He buys everything." I explained his background, his mom's house and their dogs, his work ethic, his full-time job. And then I felt angry because I had to.

"I didn't buy a VCR," I said. "I wouldn't do that."

I cried. We parked the car at the mall. The hisses and whispering stopped. I pinched my cheeks to mask the blotches so we could get out of the car. We didn't talk as we walked by Contempo Casuals and Sears and Dillard's and sat eating ice cream cones – it was silence, rocky road, and butter pecan.

She softened later that day and said, "I thought you bought it."

"I didn't."

"That's why I was upset."

"I know. But I didn't buy it."

"I want you to know why I was upset."

"I want you to know I wouldn't do that."

We went back and forth, each of us wanting something, defending something bigger than we could explain.

A month after Ron's twenty-first birthday, I called his apartment. I called his work, where they did circuit board processing with some horrible chemicals and had once had an ammonia alarm. He wasn't there either, so I knew something was wrong, and just as I started to worry, he called.

"My brother died," he said. "He was riding his bike. A drunk driver hit him and then left him there."

"I'm so sorry."

"He was only eighteen."

"I'm coming over."

"No," he said, "I need to get out of here."

He'd been sitting in his brother's room crying. When he got to my apartment, he said, "We hadn't been close like you and your brother."

He said they fought once, "I picked Jeff up and slammed him into the wall and cracked it." His voice broke, "I wish I hadn't done that. I wish I'd known we wouldn't have much time."

We went back to his mom's house. Sue was tall, with a long, elegant neck, a few gray hairs mixed into the brown. She sat, then paced, then sat again. She cooked. The dogs, Sheeba, an Irish Setter and Ron's boyhood companion, and Trixie, a lab mix, long-haired and barrel-chested, stayed close by.

I said, "I know how terrible you must feel," because I thought it was the thing to say.

"Do you?" Sue said, "Pray you never know how terrible I feel."

Joe, Ron's step-father, blew his nose, gave everyone hard hugs, and told me, "Sweetheart, I'm happy Ron has you."

A preacher visited. Ron didn't know him. The preacher told Sue that Jeff would go to hell because he hadn't been baptized, but that she could save him by her own works, and so she and Joe set about to save her son's soul.

Ron said, "We never went to church. That preacher is a vampire."

At church, where the preacher greeted us, Ron held my hand too tight. My fingers kept going numb.

I said, "You're holding my hand too tight."

He said, "I just lost my brother."

I'd only met Jeff once. He stood in the kitchen and looked unimpressed when Ron introduced us. They looked almost exactly alike and were almost exactly three years apart.

Jeff was buried in the desert in a green and manicured cemetery, his photo on the headstone, after a long funeral procession of mostly teenagers.

At the trial, the judge asked Sue what justice she'd like to see when she protested the short sentence Scott Knight was given as a repeat drunk-driving offender and now a hit-and-run driver.

She said, "I'd like to see him serve the number of years he took from my son."

The judge said, "You know that's impossible."

She spent many years doing church work, atoning for not having baptized her son. Ron fumed and stayed away.

"She's forgotten she has a living son," Ron said. "She was really cool and anti-Catholicism when we were growing up." Quite liberal, he told me. We were Republicans still, like our families, but trying on ideas, trying on the liberal identity.

A liberal mother – I imagined the possibilities.

He said, "Mom said we have to take responsibility, just like women do."

When I told him that wasn't possible, really, he said, "Not all men are bad like Joe and Paul." I said it was something else, and I tried to explain what I meant, but he said he was a good man and why did the bad men ruin it for the good ones.

When we had sex and he didn't ask first if I was taking birth control, I said, "Well, I guess I should start back on the pill." I shouldn't have laughed at the panic on his face. "Don't worry," I said, "I know I'm responsible and no man can be for me."

He didn't argue. We held each other in the dark, listening to traffic and yelling and sirens and cat fights below the stairs outside.

16. Salt River

RON AND I CONTINUED TO WORK AND GO TO SCHOOL, and I got a second job at the Information Store. We collected phone numbers to sell to solicitors, the beginning of the information age. We called 4-1-1 and asked operators for phone numbers of people named on long reams of paper, collected from government and private sources. Companies wanted every piece of contact information pieced together.

Cindy and I became friends.

"Your hair is so pretty," I said. "How did you do it?" She'd done the back comb and the hairspray just right.

She said, "Your hair is so pretty. We should go out dancing and do our hair together." We shared the same fine blond hair problem: there were girls with really big hair.

I said to Cindy, "I'm tired" as we entered data from long connected reams of computer paper.

She said, "I have something that'll give you more energy. I have a hard time getting out of my apartment every morning." Her being late wasn't really a confession. Everybody knew she was always late, but she was valuable to Tom, the owner. Cindy could fly through microfiche looking for people's personal information. I couldn't do it. It nauseated me.

Some phone operators hated us. They asked us what we were doing.

They said, "Why do you keep asking for these phone numbers?" or "Do you know this person?"

I remember one man said, "That's a horrible job. You're a terrible person."

Just like the phone soliciting job I once had in Boulder, selling newspapers and doing phone surveys – people yelled, they hung up, they questioned our character and our upbringing and our intelligence.

We were doing our job is what we always said – the obvious answer.

Cindy's boyfriend, Johnny, a carpenter, sold crystal meth for a little extra money. They took me to my first concert – AC/DC.

I don't know why I started doing meth. Maybe my propensity to negativity had something to do with thinking that snorting powder would be a good idea. Maybe it was something in my childhood. Maybe I believed it would give me more energy like Cindy said. Or maybe I wanted to expand my horizons and walk on the dangerous side of things. Or maybe it was what I looked forward to every day. Maybe it's not all that important to know why it started. It just started.

And then it had to continue, and I had to start buying it for myself. It was cheap, unlike cocaine or heroin.

Ron made fun of me at first.

Later, he said, "I'm really worried about you," while we sat in our desks before the teacher arrived. He handed me the green M&Ms from his little bag of candy – knowing the best way to avoid my irritation at receiving advice or concern was to follow it up with chocolate. I tasted chocolate and ammonia.

My boss at the domestic violence shelter said I looked terrible and couldn't focus on my job. She said, "You look like you never sleep, you're nervous, you wear the same thing every day."

I'd said to her, "I just like these clothes."

She said, "You look like shit."

At my apartment, I said to Ron, "I'm not addicted."

Ron said, "You can stop anytime you want."

At school, our friend Reagan said, "I'll do anything but I won't shoot up."

They laughed as our classmates settled in to their desks around us.

"I can stop," I said and turned away from them and drew spirals in my notebook.

Ron sat with me for hours while I wrote a computer program in the computer lab. We had to submit to the mainframe in Chicago. The TAs yelled, "Update often!" Our print compiles would come back, and we'd begin again if we had errors. Our professors talked about how fast and efficient technology had become from the punch-card days. They talked about the future, when computers would be ubiquitous. We wouldn't have to go to work. We'd work from home.

We sat waiting for a compile one day when Ron said, "I'm really worried."

I freebased with the next-door neighbor in the apartment complex. He'd been to prison for armed robbery but said it wasn't his fault and that he was clean except for this every once in a while – he said he wasn't AA clean and sober, just cutting back. The glow of the lighter in the dark room felt soothing. When I inhaled, I remembered aspen leaves quaking and gentle mountain winds – quiet and solitude. I wanted to stay in that euphoric moment, but I'd have to pay. I didn't have money beyond groceries and rent.

I had clothes and makeup because of my new Dillard's credit card. I cried when the bill came due each month, but I loved the makeup area, where well-dressed employees offered me something new – eyebrow pencil, blue mascara. I felt shame about this, despite the colors and fabrics of my new life. I'd been raised by a mother who said, "Other people have credit cards, but I don't. I own what I have. I don't owe anything."

Managing money and doing crystal and going to class and keeping up at my jobs took all my effort. I stayed in bed on days off, curtains closed.

Then I quit the job at the domestic violence shelter because the boss said, "You need to look for something else."

One morning, I woke up and knew that I couldn't make it through one day without snorting crystal. The me in the mirror spoke, "You're going to be an addict and you'll never get away from that."

I took the tiny white envelope that I'd folded, filled it with just a bit of powder. I put the rest in the toilet and flushed and took the deepest breath. I was twenty-three. *Plenty of time*, I thought, *for me to get myself together*.

Every day for a long time, I said to the mirror, "You can do this. You got out of bed and brushed your hair. You took a shower and put makeup on. You did all of that without crystal. You can get your clothes on and get into the car. If you really need it, you can have the last little bit. But if you do that, it'll be the last time you have a choice about it."

A cat walked into my apartment one day when I opened the door to go to class. She stayed the night, and in the morning there were six kittens nursing. I named her Olivia and found homes for all the kittens. She lived with me until one day she didn't return. I found her in the gutter of the five-lane Camelback Road, flattened and nearly unrecognizable.

I quit my job at the Information Store and focused only on DeVry. Mom stopped helping me with tuition, so my debt piled too fast to keep up.

And I quit Joe. I don't remember how, but I remember why. I wanted to keep Ron, but I was too late.

Ron said, "You've been seeing Joe this whole time?"

"Well, not a lot, not all the time, but yes. I never totally broke up with him."

Ron didn't speak to me for three months. At DeVry, he made wide arcs to get away from me. Once, we were walking through a doorway in opposite directions. He stopped, backed up several feet and waited for me to walk through. I was poison or a monster to him. I deserved it. He was right. He played in a band called the Dorian Blues Band. They didn't play much blues except for "Johnny, B. Goode."

Months later, I found that little white envelope. I'd forgotten about it.

Easy as that, I wasn't addicted or nearly addicted. Maybe I'd never been. Addiction had felt so permanent and impossible to escape, like Mancos, like leaving Mancos and leaving Paul, like leaving Colorado, like leaving Joe.

I went to therapy a few times. It helped. I felt less afraid. I walked to my apartment farther from the wall. I opened the curtains from time to time.

I called my father before I graduated from DeVry and said, "You missed my high school graduation, but went to Brian's. I want you to come to my college graduation."

He did. His wife, Orfita, stayed home. "She's having a terrible allergic reaction to the perfume these animals poured on her knowing she was sensitive to it. They didn't even get suspended." She'd been a crossing guard.

"Dad," I said, "You're so racist."

He laughed. "Sure," he said. "I don't think you know what racist means. You weren't around in the sixties."

I said something to Mom that I'd learned in therapy, "Family is hard for me."

The therapist told me I needed to learn how to deal with family as an adult – that it would be hard, considering the divorce and animosity, the financial issues, the distance and values. "Values, especially cause difficulty between family members because they change," he said, "over a lifetime."

Mom didn't talk much to me – I thought she was upset that I'd invited my father. She didn't talk to him at all.

Ron stopped just short of graduating, knowing all he needed about programming computers, I overheard him telling a teacher. I watched him from a distance, wondering if he'd ever talk to me again.

Before he left DeVry, he broke his silence and said, "Do you want to go to Dairy Queen?" He'd grown his hair long.

We sat down in the booth with our Blizzards – Butterfinger

and Snickers. I twisted a straw so a bubble formed that he could thump, using his thumb as a spring for his middle finger to smack the bubble, creating a loud snap. It was one of our favorite activities. He told me he was leaving because we'd broken up and it had been the only reason he'd kept going to school when he figured out there was nothing they could teach him about programming that he didn't know or couldn't figure out for himself. He said he didn't want them teaching him things that got in the way of how his own mind works. He told me we could get back together.

He said, "You can never do anything like that again."

"I won't."

I got a job at a start-up company, but the boss, a man just a few years older, wouldn't stop calling me honey and sweetie, and he stood too close and touched my shoulders and told dirty jokes and was too much over me when I sat at the computer. We worked at his home office so he could be close to his wife, who'd just had a stillbirth and was pregnant again. She had to be on bed rest.

I quit because he kept giving me less and less work, and I could see that I needed to move on. When I left, I said, "Don't call me honey."

He said, "That's why you're not working here anymore – you're going to have to toughen up if you want to work."

I'd wanted to accept it, get over it, toughen up – "How bad could it be" I told myself. I wanted to be taken seriously as an employee. The EEOC said they couldn't help me, but they made a note of it.

So, I got a job in a big corporation because there were rules about behavior and harassment and there were procedures and guidelines, and nobody called me honey and no one stood too close to me until someone did, and then he was moved to a different department.

Ron and I moved in together to an apartment with a high ceiling and a beautiful kitchen and a washer and dryer in Mesa beside the canal, the Salt River in its concrete riverbed. Our cats got along with each other – Jessica was his, Bear was mine. We made pancakes on Saturday mornings and watched our television series. We had a rhythm to our lives, a calm.

"When will we get married?" I asked because I didn't want it to turn into forever – a rhythm like this. I wanted security.

We said October. We said we'd get married in Payson, in the forest.

"BUT I DON'T want a princess wedding," I said. If I didn't have a Cinderella wedding, I would have a feminist marriage, I reasoned.

"Whatever you want, that's what we'll do," Ron said while he played video games, and I lay in the blankets I'd spread at his feet so I could be near him.

"And I don't want a blood diamond or a sweatshop dress," I said. "No one should die for my jewelry and clothes. For sure, I don't want a princess dress," I said.

I got an off-white dress that stopped at my calves – not a princess dress. I left off the veil, "The veil is virginity and purity. Did you know that in Deuteronomy it says a man can return a bride to her parents if she doesn't bleed on the sheets? So the veil is the hymen. Why do women have to bleed and suffer on their wedding night? Men don't. So sexist."

Ron didn't know. He looked sad, maybe overwhelmed.

The salesperson asked me if this were my second marriage. I asked her why she thought that and she said, "Well, the dress, you're a little older, and heavier."

"I'm twenty-five," I said.

"Yeah, well, people like us marry younger," she said. I nodded. *People like us*, I thought. She could see what I'd been trying to hide under my Dillard's card.

"I don't want my father to give me away," I said to Mom.

"Of course not," she said.

She sewed the ring pillow and was the ring bearer and the maid of honor, and I would've had her give me away and that would've made her happy, but Dad was there.

He'd called and said, "Orfita says we can't go unless I'm in the wedding because, of course, I'd do that if you wanted me to."

So, Sue and Joe, Ron's parents, walked together toward the carnation-decked arch, holding hands, then my parents walked together, not holding hands, and then it was our turn. We both remember the sun and the creek and pine trees and fresh air and the birds not singing, we believed out of deference for the moment.

We waited at the top of the steps on a dirt path, then walked to the arch and stood while the justice of the peace said the words that bound us in sickness and health and et cetera under God.

Mom didn't smile much.

Dad took photos and smiled and laughed, and Orfita sat silent – Amy, her eldest daughter, was due to have her first baby.

Brian was there and took photos – he wore a tux, his long, brown curls had grown back and were pulled down over his forehead.

We didn't want alcohol at the wedding because we didn't want to be responsible for anyone drinking and driving the narrow canyons near Payson, and we didn't want anyone drinking and driving back to Phoenix.

We had barbeque chicken and afterward sat talking on a patio with picnic benches. No music. No alcohol. Ron disappeared. Everyone left and found a local bar, and I was, suddenly and weirdly, alone and embarrassed. I found Ron, finally, in his Uncle Greg's hotel room. They'd been talking for hours.

"You're here. I was alone," I said.

Ron was surprised by my hurt and anger, "I never get to see my Uncle Greg."

Embarrassed by my selfishness and disappointment, I'd thought the wedding would be something else. I hadn't wanted a princess wedding, though. This is a good sign, I told myself – a sign that I'll have a feminist marriage.

BRIAN SERVED HIS time in the army and then he came home and lived an outdoor Colorado life. He tied flies for fishing.

Brian called and said, "I'm in the burn unit in Salt Lake City."

"Burned? What happened?"

"I was fishing and walking to where I knew I could catch a big brown trout and I fell off the edge and slid into a hot pot and broke through. I'm burned up over my ankles, almost to the knee. Water splashed up, too, and got me higher up."

"You mean…"

"No, not there."

He'd hiked off the trail and punched through the layer of earthen crust and into the boiling water below.

"I'll be there as soon as I can."

Mom couldn't get off work.

She said, "I have a lot of bills to pay." She was mad at Brian and me. She said, "I need you to pay me back. I'm in so much debt."

I told her I couldn't. "Can I pay you $100 a month?"

She said, "That won't help me. Never mind. And now Brian will have medical bills," she said as she hung up.

Dad met us at the hospital in Salt Lake. He couldn't help with the bill.

Perfect, I thought. *All those times you could've been there, and now that we don't need you, you're here.* I saw a pattern I hadn't seen before.

Dad lit a cigarette in the parking lot, and I walked away.

"I'm pregnant," I said. "Second-hand smoke can harm babies."

He laughed and said, "You and your brother are fine." He didn't put it out, but he said, "Congratulations. Boy or girl?"

"I don't know for sure because we don't need to know. We'll be happy either way."

But we knew she was a girl. Ron had a dream of a daughter. I felt her daughterness – no other way to describe it. Friends said, "You have to have a girl." Ron's mom said, "You'll have a boy. Cox men don't make girls. Remember that if you have a girl, it's not your fault – the male's contribute the gender."

Brian came to Phoenix to live with Ron and me. He spent a

while reading, recovering, and waiting for the burns to heal. I supplied him with beer and chewing tobacco and rubbed the burn lotion into the skin he couldn't reach – it caused him great pain. He tied some flies and dreamed of having his own business. And he wrote about river raft guiding on the Gunnison River and about Colorado.

We were both in a state of cocooning – waiting for another phase of life, our skins changing. I loved being pregnant – my belly was beautiful to everyone then. I could breathe out.

He said he was going to break up with his girlfriend, Kelley. "She's too religious. She thinks it's her duty to change me, to save me."

I didn't want to be changed either. I told Ron, "I don't want to change my name and I don't want to hyphenate our names because our child will just drop mine in the end anyway. None of this is right especially when I'm the one having the baby."

Ron said, "Well, I can't take your name."

"Why not?"

He said, "If I take your name, it'll be just as bad as your having to take mine."

I didn't have the words then to explain why he was wrong, so I decided to let it go.

Ever the student of culture, Mom told me about other naming traditions in the world, so we decided we'd choose a new name for both of us.

Ron said, "Since I'm willing to change my name, can I choose it?"

"Sure," I said.

He came back some days later with our name.

He said, "Forrester. Our son – if we have a son, some day, will be named Rook. Rook Forrester."

Before the official name change, Ron got a letter from a lawyer – it was a request from a woman in California seeking child support from the father of her child. Ron Forrester was the name of that father, so my husband got a letter as did other men named

Ron Forrester. I was only a couple of months away from delivery, so when Ron and I showed up in the lawyer's office, her eyes were huge. We explained Ron had only ever been with me and that he hadn't been in California since 1989.

The lawyer took his photo and said, "Don't worry about this. It's obviously not you."

Friends of mine said, "How do you know, for sure?"

"I know," I said. "I trust him. He'd never cheat."

Ron and I sat in the courtroom waiting for our turn, listening to the judge preside over other name change petitions. He didn't hesitate over the requests of various people who'd been convicted of crimes and who were now sure their new identity would redeem them, which seemed hopeful and beautiful – they could begin again. The judge approved no matter how many other aliases and no matter how many crimes.

When it was our turn, he looked at me. "What is this you're doing with your names?" the judge said, looking over the top of his glasses, his slick black hair unmoving as he tilted his face forward. "Why didn't you just change your name when you got married?"

We explained several times. I explained that there are many different customs around the world to name a new family. He blinked at me and looked at Ron and said, "What's wrong with your father's name?"

Ron said he hadn't seen his father since he was ten.

"I want to be a different kind of father," he said.

The judge sighed and shrugged and gave us our new name, shaking his head as he signed the papers, sitting in his heavy wooden pulpit in that heavy wooden courtroom.

Brian left Phoenix, having shed most of his burned skin.

And then it was my turn to come out of my chrysalis.

We chose two names, just in case. My parents didn't have a name for me when I was born because they'd assumed I'd be a boy. "It didn't occur to us that we'd have a girl," Mom had told me.

If I had a boy, his name would be Jeffrey Brian – after our

brothers. If I had a girl, she'd be Chiara – a name we found in the baby name book and knew was right the moment we read it.

At one point, I panicked over it, "What if it's too different?" I said. "Maybe we should change it."

Ron said, "No. That's her name."

A doctor said, "That's how yuppies name their babies – they go through the baby name book."

I said, "But it was awesome – both of us said, 'That's it,' at the same time."

The doctor said, "It's a very pretty name."

"It's Italian," I said.

I BREATHED THE go-away-pain breath. The Pitocin dripped. I was going to meet my baby soon.

The Smashing Pumpkins played "Today" – "Today is the greatest."

In the haze of adrenaline and pain and painkillers and childbirth, I told Ron I understood things.

"It all comes down to this moment."

He was huddled in the corner, afraid of all the suffering. I told him that it was okay, nothing I couldn't face, and I knew that now. I was so happy.

As I breathed, the adrenaline rushed and raced and swirled and I was back in time when I used to run the country roads, the long winding gravel roads, the skinny paved roads, the dirt path, the empty fields. I was free then. And I ran and ran. Not fast or strong, but free in solitude, I felt a real kind of power. All I needed was my two feet and open space, and I had all that.

I ran back into the present, and with one more massive push, met Chiara.

Big bright blue eyes, wispy halo bit of hair. She looked straight into me.

We were born right then, in that moment, born of high elevation Colorado breath and glacial peaks and narrow whitewater rivers and wide desert sky and hope for more compassion, less violence, and something more – solitude. Freedom. I wanted to give her something I'd received.

Her name fit her – it means clear and bright.

I'D BEEN PREPARING to tell Mom that I could do things without her. I read a dozen parenting books, but when Chiara was born I wanted Mom to stay forever, but she had to get back to work. She'd found a job in Edwards, where we'd lived in the trailer park in the doublewide with our father. She lived in a singlewide in Dotsero, near the confluence of the Eagle and Colorado Rivers. She skied and hiked on the weekends, returning to the mountains and rivers of our young childhood – Gold Peak and Lions Head and the Eagle River.

"I left out of shame," she said. "I never wanted to leave the Vail Valley. People had always liked your father – he was a good skier, people liked his stories."

I called Mom every few days for weeks. There was colic.

I cried into the phone to Mom, "What do I do?"

She quoted Shakespeare, and for the first time ever, I understood and wasn't annoyed. "This above all: to thine own self be true."

She sent me an article about parenting without spanking. She said, "The only reason people spank is because they're angry, and they don't know what else to do."

When Chiara was crying in public I'd get dirty looks, worried glances, unsolicited and loud advice about how to make my baby stop crying. I worked at the credit card processing center in the technology support department – turned things off and back on, mostly, then went home to colic, tried to sleep a few hours between bouts of colic, went to work. Repeat. I was satisfied when the baby cried less – there was so little I could do to stop the colic and what seemed to be such suffering.

Ron knew we needed something. He said, "At first, you're gonna hate it, but then you'll like it."

That was the hint that I got about where Ron wanted to take the baby and me.

He said to wear comfortable shoes and that I didn't have to dress up.

I wasn't sure he knew what he was doing.

We drove north, and he stopped at the side of the highway, rolled into a turn-off and parked. We got out and walked through the darkness, navigating rocks and cactus, the thin sliver of moon and the light-bubble still enveloping us – we weren't that far from home, but far enough that the city let us go, and I could breathe.

We walked on. I heard water. We passed broken glass and cans – a party spot.

Later, we sat on the banks of the Salt River, a precious desert river.

"You were right," I told Ron, "At first I hated this. And now, I'm very happy."

"I know you," he said.

We sat listening to the water between the stones and along the sand.

I started to remember again rivers and where I'd come from after spending so much time and emotion on forgetting what I'd been and learned and forgetting what I'd fought against without knowing why. I'd been pushing memory away, not wanting what I'd learned of blood and animal tendon and how it comes away from bone and what I'd learned of violence and the hatred of sensitivity. I'd been severed from wilder rivers wanting to become something other than Mancos. Something other than a small-town girl.

The Salt River, a stream most of the time in the Sonoran Desert, whispered to me to return to the source of what no drug, no man, no circumstance can kill.

Chiara was calm and didn't cry.

v. The Wildness of the Source You Can't Kill

17. My Chevy S10 Pickup Truck

I LOADED MY BLACK CHEVY S10 PICKUP TRUCK WITH life-sized, red-painted plywood silhouettes representing women and their children killed as a result of domestic violence, most often murdered by men – boyfriends, husbands, domestic partners.

I drove the silhouettes from place to place – university events, women's organization meetings, parks, and malls. The National Organization for Women (NOW) chose me to speak for them because they said, "You're young and pretty and you have time. People listen to pretty people."

A newspaper reporter and a television reporter interviewed me as I walked among the silhouettes and the shadows they cast under the Arizona sun on the grass outside our apartment. I read the names and stories of the women and talked about the hope for the Silent Witness Project – more awareness, fewer deaths. The reporters said they could cut out the vocal pauses and nervous laughter.

The camera panned from my blue-painted toenails and sandaled feet to the red silhouette feet as I read aloud, "Theresa was a loving mother of two. She threw her boyfriend out and was ending the relationship when he returned and killed her. The perpetrator was convicted of first-degree murder and sentenced to life in prison."

The camera panned to her shadow.

A church with a massive cross pointing into the desert sky above Scottsdale invited us to speak and to set up the silent witnesses outside next to the white rock yard planted with prickly pear cactus, yucca, and palo verde.

The reverend asked what I wanted to say to his congregation and then took a seat close by. I stepped to the podium, afraid I'd get the "ums," but a miracle occurred.

I looked out and saw men in all their power sitting with families in a church, and I felt a strange, deep anger, and a thought flashed lightning and thunder to my tongue.

I said, "People always ask me, 'Why does she stay with him?' but they never ask, 'Why does he hit her if he loves her?'"

I looked at the reverend as he nodded his head and said, "Good question," and motioned me back to my seat.

I'd sent Mom a picture of my long, pregnancy-vitamin-infused fingernails, a dig at her for spanking me for seeking sympathy as a child over a broken nail.

"I'm thin, too. I love the breast-feeding diet," I said on the phone.

"Hmm," she said. I wanted her to believe me and tell me I was beautiful by her standards, even though she couldn't really see me, but she sounded distracted and didn't mention my nails. She said she remembered the breast-feeding diet as a helpful thing.

I sent Mom a copy of the newspaper article and told her about being on television and about the project and the NOW meetings.

She said, "You've always been a joiner."

I said, "No! I really believe in this. What do you mean a joiner?"

She laughed and didn't answer.

"I believe in this," I said.

She told me she had a season pass to ski at Vail, and then said, "I hope you don't mind that all I leave you is a bunch of debt."

"It's good, Mom. You deserve a season pass," I said. "I'm glad you're back there again."

Ron and I had our own debt. After three years of seeing

envelopes from the IRS stamped in red ink, addressed to Ron, that he never opened, I opened one he got during our fourth year of marriage – the words OVERDUE and IRS on the same envelope terrified me. I hadn't opened them because they were his. We respected each other's privacy – a way to prove our trust. "I'll do it, I promise," he said, but they never got taken care of. We owed four years of back taxes when our baby was six months old.

We moved to a tiny apartment without a washer and dryer in Phoenix, close to North Mountain, a piece of unpaved desert in the middle of the ever-expanding city. I took the baby hiking there, sitting on my hip, tied in a paisley wrap. We looked for the coyotes we heard every night as they hunted and howled through the urban alleys, raiding the cat population. Sometimes we heard cat death screams. We walked up the mountain past creosote and Mormon tea, saw horny toads and lizards and snakes and quail and hummingbirds and the rare roadrunner. Chiara pointed at the desert world and spoke to it in her baby language.

Mom and I went to twelve-step meetings because it was the nineties and we belonged to a shame-based culture. We discussed our meetings because anonymity issues didn't apply to us. I went to Overeaters Anonymous, and she went to Co-Dependents Anonymous because nothing else really fit her.

I told Mom that someone in a meeting said, "No one can make you feel angry."

Mom said, "I can't feel angry in a vacuum."

"True," I said. "Really true."

Chiara woke in her crib and I said, "Hold on a minute, gotta get the baby."

I held her on my hip and fed her peas from my palm as I walked the short length of the hallway.

I got Chiara to laugh between bites of peas, and Mom laughed hearing the baby laugh, then she got quiet and said, "I'm not controlling, am I, because there's a guy at my CoDA meeting who says I am."

"You were only controlling when you had to be," I said.

"Hmm, that's interesting. Tell me more."

I told her about the times she told us what to wear, what to eat, when to do our homework, what to say, what not to say.

"These, Mama, are things that moms are supposed to do."

She said, "Well, why does this guy keep saying that to me after I share?"

"Because he's an asshole, Mom, or maybe he likes you and he's trapped in middle school."

She didn't laugh. She was annoyed because I said "asshole."

She said, "Maybe he does like me. He's attractive. My therapist says that I'm afraid of commitment."

"You're afraid of commitment to a bad person, but you're not afraid of commitment. Think about your life and everything you've done."

She laughed, "Maybe you're right about being afraid of commitment to a bad person. I sure didn't want to marry again after your dad."

"I can imagine," I said.

"You know he said to me at your graduation that I did a good job with you kids with no help from him."

"Wow," I said. "Good he knows that."

She said, "He has no idea. He doesn't mean what he says. A long time ago, he said he wanted to keep the family together, but he only likes the idea of family, not actual family."

We had Thanksgiving at Ron's parents' house in Phoenix.

Mom brought her traditional apple-nut bread, but sat down late to dinner because she'd played the give-up-your-seat-and-earn-travel-miles game. I was angry.

"I can't believe she's late," I said to Ron.

To her I said, "I wanted you to be here, but you wanted to save money."

Lips pursed, she shook her head, and I felt ashamed. Of course she should save money. She'd raised us, struggling with money. It was still the same as when we were young – we were ever-navigating "how could you" and "not supposed to."

But then she said, "Why do you mind, anyway? You say family is difficult for you."

I tried to explain that she wasn't just "family" – she was more, I told her, but too late for her feelings to recover. I wished I could take the words back, that I'd counted to ten.

Ron's mom, born and raised in Indiana, made one of her traditional Midwest foods – sweet potato casserole with corn flakes and brown sugar crumble and marshmallows. Mom had turned her back on the Midwest food culture, exchanging granola and yogurt for baked tuna noodle casserole topped with potato chips.

Brian brought his girlfriend, Kelley, red-haired and from Grand Junction. He hadn't broken up with her yet.

Chiara was eight months old.

We talked about Tonya Harding and Nelson Mandela. "Well, good that Apartheid is over," Mom said, and everyone nodded. We talked about other relatives – Ron's cousin was in jail again, but seemed to be doing better, "Taking more responsibility for his actions." We talked about how Chiara had trouble sleeping. "You just have to make sure she knows it's time to sleep. You have to be consistent with your expectations," was the consensus from Ron's parents and Brian and Kelley, borrowing the words of Kelley's mother's expertise after four children. Mom said, "You were a fussy baby, too. Brian could sleep through anything." We talked about our lives, jobs, and schools – Brian and Kelley were in college or had been or would be. Education would help us all with our jobs – we'd take on debt or we had and would do it again. Brian said he couldn't get a degree in journalism, "because they try to tell you how to think. They try to make you a liberal."

Ron's mom laughed when Chiara opened her mouth as I put a bite of stuffing into my mouth. She said, "Oh, poor Chiara, she wanted that food, and you ate it instead." She laughed and said, "Wait'll I tell her that when she's older."

"No. Don't. I'm so embarrassed. Don't ever tell that story again," I said. Inarticulate, defensive, ashamed. I pulled Chiara closer.

Sue said, "You should've seen her face. I just think it's a funny story."

"It's not funny. It sounds like I didn't feed her, but I fed myself."

Mom changed the subject, rescued me, adept as she'd always been at polite conversation.

Later, because I'd been upset, Ron said, "My mom used to be so cool, honey. I wish you'd known her before Jeffrey died. She listened to us. She was so different."

Mom sent an email later defending Sue over my discomfort about her joke that I fed myself instead of Chiara. She wrote, "There's nothing worse than losing a child."

I was humiliated by it all – that I didn't allow a grieving mother a funny story at my expense. I wanted my daughter to grow up knowing I'd feed her before I fed myself.

Mom had a bilingual education conference in Phoenix when Chiara was about a year old.

We sat on the carpet in the apartment by the sliding glass doors and drank Kahlua. The moon shone through a palm tree. We were pulling from a deck of animal cards designed to give readings similar to Tarot cards, the accompanying book explained our metaphors. One spread would show us how we see ourselves or how others see us.

Mom said, "Let's avoid that one."

We laughed and decided to do the Butterfly Spread, which could foresee the outcomes of projects.

"What's your project?" I said, but she wouldn't tell me.

In the dark with our drinks, we talked. I had my Kahlua with milk and ice, but Mom had hers straight. She didn't want the extra calories.

The animal cards made me think how Mom had a gift for seeing animals. Once, she and Brian came home from hiking in the La Plata Mountains. Brian had been about fourteen at the time.

"We heard a bear," she said.

Wide-eyed jealous, I said, "That's so lucky!"

"No," she said, "We heard the roar unlike anything I'd ever imagined. The bear was between us and the van."

"So, what did you do?"

"We had to get back to the van. No other choice. We walked toward it and hoped the bear would walk away from, not toward, us."

"Why didn't you make a lot of noise?" I said. "You know you have to make a lot of noise so they know where you are."

"I'm glad you weren't there."

I said something she already knew so she was glad I hadn't been there.

I felt a separation of my tissues, an ache in my veins, a leaking pain. It wasn't a new thing I'd done, had some know-it-all detail to share. I did this all the time. I wished I didn't have so many opinions, that I didn't have such a need to speak, to find holes, to figure things out, to know everything there was to know. I felt ashamed of my detail-finder, my ever-moving tongue.

I took a long drink of my Kahlua to gather myself.

Mom noticed and changed the subject and said, "You'll be so happy with me. I've been voting like a Democrat, so I just went ahead and changed my party."

I smiled, "You're a Democrat."

She said, "Don't tell your brother." We smiled at each other. The ice in my drink cracked. Wind blew the long, white vertical blinds.

"Will Kelley and I get along?" I said. "It was hard to tell at Thanksgiving."

Mom said, "Hmm. I don't know."

"Why?"

"She's very religious," Mom said.

"Maybe I can keep my opinions to myself," I said.

We startled the baby awake with our laughter. I took her out of her crib and we sat on the floor together. Chiara handed us cards after drooling on them. We pulled three cards for her: Dog – loy-

alty/keep the right company; Frog–transformation/self-protec-
tion; Dragonfly–illusion as power/power as illusion.

Mom went home a day later, after the bilingual conference
ended. Chiara and I waved at her plane as it took off.

Mom emailed me the list of animals she saw. I emailed:
Elk–stamina/stress; porcupine–innocence/warning; bear–intro-
spection/intuition.

She saw a golden eagle soaring over the river. "It seemed
significant," she said.

I consulted the text.

The book said "the eagle is the connection to the divine,"
and it said something about freedom.

She emailed back that she'd send a longer note later, that
she was busy making plans. She typed, "Crom!"

We talked on the phone on her fifty-fourth birthday. Chiara,
not yet a year and a half old, played in a tiny plastic baby pool on
the balcony while I sat watching her.

Mom said, "I decided to build a house in Gypsum."

Gypsum was across the highway from Dotsero.

"That'll be good."

"It's the farthest up the valley I could get."

The valley had filled up during the last decades with Californians, Texans, Nevadans wanting to get away from civilization
by moving to the mountains.

The house she intended to have built would have five extra
rooms–one for her aunt, Elsa, in Florida who she wanted to have
come live with her, one for a sewing room. "Maybe I can rent the
others out."

We talked about Brian and his rafting job and his girlfriend.

She said, "Someday, he'll make a good father."

"I can't imagine him as a father," I said, but she didn't answer.

"Anyway," she said, "everything is in storage. I'm renting a
room in a coworker's house. She's a teacher at Edwards Elementary, too. I'm not sure I'm getting a season pass. I'd thought about
it, but I haven't decided."

She asked about the baby and Ron. I said, "It's hard right now. He works a lot, but I also like that he always has a job."

"Oh," she said.

"We didn't want to put her in daycare so we swapped schedules and didn't see each other. I quit my job so we can spend more time together. It was just too hard." I didn't tell her about our debt problems and that daycare was expensive and that after the math, it all seemed to come out the same in the end.

I told her I felt pressure to have another baby. "People don't want Chiara to be an only child. I don't know. I think she'll be fine."

I told her what felt good in my life. Ron, ever generous with his money, said I made it possible for him to make the money he made, trusted my mothering, read me to sleep on the nights we were home together when I had trouble sleeping.

She said, "Have you read *The Cinderella Complex* yet? I really think you should."

"I'm not a Cinderella, Mom," my throat filled with stones. Chiara wanted to be picked up then, so I walked and bounced her while I kept talking.

She changed the subject, "I'm going diving in Mexico – I leave in three days.

"Who are you going to Mexico with?"

"I'm going alone, and don't end your sentences with prepositions."

Irritated, I said, "Mom."

"It'll be fine," she said, irritated by my worry. I had reasons to worry, though.

Recently, she'd told me about a man she didn't trust who had been harassing her at work. "He's a creep, but I don't know how to tell him that I can't go out with him."

"Mama, you tell him no."

Chiara grabbed at the phone, wanting to talk into it as we stood outside on the balcony, hummingbirds buzzing us, while seeking flowers in the parched desert of pavement, concrete, and adobe.

"But your reputation is everything and if you get the reputation that you're a – um, a bitch…" She said the word *bitch* as if it were a live thing. I thought it was about time she started adding cuss words to her vocabulary.

I interrupted, "Be a bitch, Mom. Who cares about reputation."

"It's the most important thing…"

I interrupted again, "No, Mom. You're the most important thing. You don't have to do things you don't want to do. People will think what they want anyway."

"Oh, Jeffy," I heard her disappointment. I felt it, too, and then some.

Always interrupting. Always having some opinion.

A hummingbird flew past, hunting chuparosa flowers and ocotillo.

She scuba dived quite a bit. She dove the Blue Hole, she dove off the coast of Florida, she dove in Mexico with Sheck, her boyfriend at the time. He'd been a cave diver. Only the specially trained went cave diving or deep diving, she'd explained to me. He'd been an expert. And he'd died. "I do miss him, but I think I miss more the idea of him." I thought she'd say something else, but she went on, "I'm not wanting to marry anyone anyway. Not getting into that mess again, as you know."

She laughed and said, "But you'll be fine being married." I'd never be the woman she'd been. We both knew that. Still, my feelings were hurt.

After a moment, she said, "There's something I want to say to you, Jeffy." She paused. I gathered myself for something. "Whether you have a relationship with your father or not, it's not your fault what happened or what will happen with him. I want you to be free of that." The next day, I got a package for the baby in the mail from her – socks and a onesie – Colorado Rockies – the baseball team. I added it to the collection of Colorado sports team baby apparel. Mom sent Broncos stuff to Ron for Christmas as a joke between them. He would never be a Broncos fan, he said. She begged to differ and said she wouldn't rest until he reformed.

18. Up to Leadville

I LISTENED TO THE VOICEMAIL MESSAGE AGAIN. "THIS is the American Consulate in Mexico. We are trying to reach Jenny, daughter of Judith." The voice left a phone number to write down and call back.

I called the consulate number and had to leave a message. I missed their call back.

Then the phone range, and I said hello.

"It's your Uncle John." He said, "Jenny, something's happened to your mom."

"Is she okay?"

Time passed.

"No," he said it softly, not wanting to say it.

I scrambled to hope. "Will she be okay?"

More time spent itself. He put the word down even more softly, even as hard a word as it is.

"No. I'm sorry, Jenny. She's. She died." His voice cracked. He'd been to Vietnam. I'd never heard his voice crack.

He didn't know the details.

Chiara wanted to practice walking on the stairs, but I had to stay by the phone attached to the wall. Then I called Brian. He was out, they said, "On the river." Someone would have to bring him in so that I could tell him what had happened.

Brian said, "I think I should stay out here instead of going to the funeral. That's the way she'd want it."

"She would probably want you at her funeral."

"She'd want me out here where she is, where she taught me to be."

"Yeah, but you gotta come to the funeral. She'd understand that, too."

"Yeah, okay."

The American Consulate representative in Mexico and I talked. There'd been a diving accident. There was an issue of money. The man said things could be delicate when returning bodies to their home countries, but if I had $2,500 things would go more smoothly. I borrowed the money from Uncle John.

From what we pieced together from phone calls with the consulate representative and a local dive store owner and from a newspaper article, Mom had met some people in a hotel. They decided to go cave diving. They entered a cenote, a sinkhole. Inland fresh waters and ocean waters blend into haloclines as the tides push in and away again through the dark and narrow lime-stone passages.

There are two smaller holes in the limestone ring and a larger ring, where the sun shines down into the sinkhole. Look-ing up from the water, you see two eyeholes and the gaping maw of the cenote's namesake, the skull – La Calavera.

If there'd been light inside the water-filled cave, the water would have been bright blue against the white walls. The stalag-mites and stalactites like vampire's teeth. The only times Mom woke from her nightmares screaming in my childhood, there'd been vampires.

A young man who called himself a dive guide had taken this group of people into a water-filled cave, passed a sign warning of the danger, and into a passage called the Madonna. He didn't check on them for forty-five minutes. When he did check on them they were gone, and he was alone.

A Danish man died, though his two companions survived. They escaped, holding their breaths and kicking at the ghosts behind them.

The wife of the man who owned the dive store and oxygen

tanks died. She'd been resuscitated but died in route to the hospital. Her husband chickened out last minute and didn't take his place as the last person in the group, responsible for those ahead of him. He didn't tell anyone. He swam back out of the cave with a bad feeling and sat at the edge of the limestone ring, waiting.

An Italian man escaped, too.

And an Englishman.

But Mom lost her way in the cave. Her single light went out, and in that dark cave she couldn't find her way. She removed her mask, a last attempt to find air somewhere. It took them almost two hours to find her.

Mom knew about cave diving and its dangers. Sheck had died deep-sea diving, tied to the rope that was his lifeline. The gases he mixed to force his lungs to greater depths didn't work the way they always had. Something had gone wrong and he'd known it so he wrapped the rope around his arm so the body could be retrieved. It was generous of him to solve the mystery for the people he left behind. But even Sheck hadn't taken her cave diving. Too dangerous.

I called Ron at work and ever seeking the cause and meaning of things, said, "She followed Sheck's ghost into the cave. I need you to come, please, to take care of everything."

During our phone conversation, Uncle John said, "You know, this isn't the first call from an American consulate that we've gotten about your mom."

When she was nineteen, she traveled in Mexico with friends in her VW van. A friend had been driving while Mom slept in the back of the van, her head pointed toward the front. A collision caused her to slam into the back seat. She woke up in the hospital with a head injury that required medical attention for several weeks. Her father and brother got that consulate phone call.

That night, after all the phone calls, I heard the crib gate slam down. I went to check, but it was fine. But I knew. My mama had taken the baby out to play and held her up to the light coming through the window.

Ron took care of Chiara while I went to Colorado to take care of Mom's land and her belongings and to tend to her burial after her body was flown from Mexico and taken up to Leadville, the closest mortuary. I stayed in her rented room in her friend's house in the mountains, where bears visited while people soaked in the hot tub. I drank too much wine and read Mom's diving magazines.

The list of precautions for cave diving were clear.

Reserve a minimum of two-thirds of your air for your exit.

Bring plenty of light – don't depend on one light.

Lay your own line – don't depend on the lines already laid down by previous divers.

Don't go too deep, and don't go beyond the limits of your training.

Mom's group included too many divers. They broke every rule.

Uncle John, his wife, and I drove up the mountain from Edwards, filled then with hotels and golf courses.

When we past the farm turned plant nursery and business mall, and I remembered Uncle John wanting to give his small, adopted son a hundred spanks, I wanted to hug my cousin for having survived. When my cousin was young, he was what we called "effeminate." Uncle John had tried to beat the gay out of him.

Uncle John, Aunt Barb, and I passed the grocery store where I stole candy and Mom made me apologize. We passed the house by the movie theater – the first one we'd lived in after I was born.

We passed the bend where Uncle John ran his jeep off the road and pulled over at the next narrow mountain highway shoulder and looked down. His jeep had landed on a ledge. If he'd missed that ledge, he would've hurtled hundreds of feet to the bottom of the canyon into the raging Eagle River.

Uncle John said, "I made it through two tours in Vietnam, and this road almost killed me."

I asked him if anyone had spoken against him, said anything cruel to him, when he returned from Vietnam. He said no one did, and if they had, if they hadn't believed what he'd been through, it would have hurt him.

Uncle John once said, "All young people should have to go into the military to see how little they really matter." I was surprised he'd needed to go into the military to find that out.

We stood a while in the wind, not wanting to get where we had to go any faster than necessary.

When we got to the funeral home, we stood by the casket. Aunt Barb didn't go in with us. She'd lost five relatives that year.

Uncle John said, "You're not coming?" His eyebrows high, his face in a hard frown.

"I just can't handle any more death," she said.

Uncle John said, "Can't handle any more?" He shook his head and laughed a hurt laughter. "Geezus," he said under his breath.

When we got to Mom's casket in that small, wood-paneled room filled with caskets at 10,000 feet in elevation, I saw her surrounded by pioneer ghosts sitting on their haunches, too exhausted to look up from under their bonnets, dead babies in their arms. I heard the swishing of pebbles in hopeful mining pans – Leadville, the home of gold hunters. The mountains made of stone and money.

Uncle John and I held hands by the metal casket. I cried. He blew his nose – the way a man like him cries.

Afterward, we walked around the tourist town. We hadn't walked there together for over two decades. I told him I wanted to make sure I grieved properly because I'd read that if you don't grieve properly, you carry your grief into the rest of your life.

He said with his Minnesota accent, his war and weather-hewn voice, "Well, I think you're doing a fine job grieving."

When I was three or four, Mom and I stood in front of a window in Leadville. A pioneer mannequin woman held a basket of dry goods in one arm and the hand of her daughter as they stood by a wagon in the wilderness with the Rocky Mountains rising behind them, a long line of wagons streaming down.

"Someday, I'll be the mama and you'll be the daughter," I told her.

Before Mom's funeral and before the backhoe dug the hole for the coffin, when I slept the nights before in her rented room, in her bed, wanting her to seep into me and not to lose her, I read more of her journals, seeking to know her thoughts, to find something to hold onto.

She wrote about my being overweight again as a nightmare she'd had. I cried rage at her. My body, one of my ever-expanding and contracting bodies, gave her nightmares even after seeing my struggles, the despair, the giving up, the going on, the living in a fat body – the jeers, the exclusion, the assumptions, the awful and ironic invisibility.

She wrote about Vern. She said, "You hurt me in your truck." I hadn't known. Mom and I had this in common – pain at the hands of men on dark roads.

I remembered the time I made sure Mom stood beside me when Star Trek came on with the introduction was changed to "To boldly go where no one has gone before." "Wait'll you hear this," I said, so excited.

She said, "No! They still split the infinitive."

"They got rid of the sexism," I yelled, eyes rolling to the starry rural sky and said, "You're obsessed with grammar."

"You're obsessed with feminism," she said. She had meant it to hurt.

I'd wanted to be understood, to close a gap between us – to be together in some struggle, some reality I knew we shared financially, emotionally, but she'd lived so many years alone inside her worries and keeping her own counsel. If I'd had the words, I would've told her I wasn't a joiner – that my obsession with feminism came from the words "boys will be boys" and from the Second Amendment and from trying to leave our small town and from hunger and never being thin enough.

I looked through her checkbook – she just bought tires for Brian, home from the service, struggling.

What would *he* do without her?

What would we do?

MOM HAD JUST gotten a loan to buy land to build the house she'd told me she wanted to build. A square patch of earth beside the railroad track in Gypsum, Colorado, stood vacant and would continue to stand vacant now.

I stood on one corner of the lot with a slick-haired man who said, "Your mom told me she could get a mortgage of $300 a month. I didn't believe anyone could do that, but your mom had figured it out."

"So, what do we do with it now?"

"Well, no money's exchanged hands. The paperwork had barely started. You got $40,000? I could give it to you now."

"Oh." The ownership of this Colorado blue sky and the view of the deep red volcano across the valley was beyond me.

"Tell you what. I'll sell it for you. No charge."

The debt felt like fishing line tightening, pulling on a sharp hook. College, credit cards, unpaid federal taxes.

Mom used to collect home-building catalogues. Brian and I would choose our favorite, knowing that we'd never really get a house.

Mom and I had talked a lot about God because of the twelve-step programs. She'd told me, "If you name It God, you make It too small."

Maybe it was the same kind of thing with the idea of home. If you try to build it out of wood and put it in one place, or when you own and fence it, you make it too small.

The preacher was a normal kind of man, a friend of our mom's. He asked to do the funeral and said he knew about Mom and about us and our eclectic ideas about religion. Said he thought he could do right by our mom and by us.

We said yes, but we wanted some things said and didn't want others said.

I sat in her classroom at Edwards Elementary School, where

she was the ESL teacher. I found a stash of unsalted sunflower seeds and a freezer bag full of plastic bread ties – she used them for counting. I'd sent her mine by the envelope-full. A staff meeting was happening across the hall from her room – school was about to begin again. There was a surge of laughter. I got up and closed the door. One of her coworkers came over and cried with me.

The principal asked if the memorial could be at the school. She said, "You weren't the only ones who lost someone. She was very important to this school, to this community, especially the Spanish-speaking community here."

We gathered in the grassy field outside the school in the valley carved by the Eagle River under the soon-to-be-white-capped peaks, the trailer park we'd lived in after the farm was sold, not far away. The mountains where we'd roamed like they belonged to us, and we'd belonged to them, everything still and silent.

My baby girl, in her finest burgundy dress wouldn't let me put her down. She cried every time I tried. I held her, feeling hollow and weak, and she pulled me through the memorial by the force of her own tiny, formidable will.

Friends from different decades of Mom's life talked to us.

Gail, a friend of hers from the Vail days, said, "Your mom used to tell me I was brave because I traveled alone to Israel to visit family and friends there, but your mom was the brave one. I could return home to my husband and my house. Your mom didn't have those things and she traveled anyway. She was the kind of brave that most people aren't. She was a good example for you and your brother."

At the gravesite, the pallbearers lifted the casket and set it down by the open grave while the preacher's words came into the air and went somewhere.

I thought about the things I now knew about Vern in that moment when he lifted one corner of our mom's casket. I'd laid awake with those journals that held her darkest thoughts. Vern wasn't just a small-town logger who took us hunting and taught us to drive a stick shift and laughed at me when I cried over dying deer we'd shot. He'd used his strength against my mother in their private moments.

The preacher said the funeral isn't for the dead but for the living, so when Vern picked up a corner of her casket to place her in the earth, I wanted to shout out his crimes against my mother – to claim some kind of justice. He'd given too much to her to bear with his "it's not that bad" when he hurt her feelings and "Oh, don't get hissy," when she got mad. He'd left her lonely because he was ashamed that Mom didn't belong to his religion, holding her at arm's length.

Vern wore a tie and a jacket.

His best cowboy boots were shined.

I couldn't find the right words or the right moment – I knew my brother would be angry and wouldn't understand. He hadn't read what I'd read. He didn't hear things the same way either.

Chiara played in the pile of reddish brown dirt – rich and dark. She wanted her shoes off, so I held them in my lap. She talked to herself and laughed and dug her fingers in and brushed them off, small hands rubbing together, clapping. Then she got up to go sit in my grandmother's lap, who was my dad's mother, but then didn't want to be picked up – restless. She tottered and toppled inches from that six-foot-deep hole.

Among us, pupils dilated. Every breath sucked in, then vowels escaped as we watched the littlest of us get too close to that hole, that space. I picked her up and hugged her close, she pushed away, "No, want down," she said. I had to put her down. I'd have many things to let go of.

I saw things that had been lost. Chiara would never know her grandma, the woman who raised chickens among bobcats and milked goats in the freezing Colorado Rockies. She'd never hear her grandma play the organ, and she'd never hear her grandma sing. She'd never know that her grandma defied her family because she divorced, without a reason good enough for them, and then defied a whole town because she never found a good enough reason to marry, and yet was the kindest and sweetest of all of us. Chiara needed to know that kind of true rebellion. I didn't think she'd learn it from me.

There were things I knew I'd hold onto, reach for, make up, create, invent, keep. Words were born in that moment. I'd write in the journal. I'd write my questions until I found answers or peace.

The grave marker was etched with an eagle soaring above the words, "Her spirit outran her body. Grandmother, mother, sister, friend, and teacher. We were lucky to be her children."

When we went home to Phoenix, I got sympathy cards addressed to, "Mr. and Mrs. Ron Forrester." I sure hadn't seen that coming, the erasure of my carefully constructed name.

I sat with the cards, opening them and reading stories people told about her. For a while, I walked in the world seeing everyone as if they'd die tomorrow. Maybe they would. That clarity and love wore off, though – it was too large a perspective to hold while also washing dishes and paying bills and keeping up.

I was in the Denver airport and ran into Mrs. Weaver from church in Mancos. We'd spent holidays and many Sundays together. The Weaver Ranch cattle dotted the green valley meadows along the Mancos River. Mr. Weaver was a smiling man with beautiful wrinkled eyes.

She'd heard about Mom and had an obituary written, requesting funds to be paid to us, but the banker said no one donated, saying, "I guess she'd left the area too long ago, and no one remembered her." Mrs. Weaver and I talked for a long time about things that had changed and things that had stayed the same.

She was walking away and stopped and said to me, "Do you remember what you said when we helped you three move into the trailer?"

I didn't.

"You told me that if you hadn't had so many stuffed animals, your dad wouldn't have been so mad at you and your parents wouldn't have gotten divorced."

"Oh." I looked out at the Denver airport landscape and noticed it was the same now as the day I'd left Colorado for Arizona and had hugged Mom and said that I'd be back even though we both knew that I'd left for good.

Mrs. Weaver, said, "I just wanted to tell you that so you don't have to carry it around anymore."

AFTER MOM DIED, people said to me, "There's a reason for everything." Christians, Buddhists, pagans, everybody said this in their own way. I despised them for it.

Her big red dive bag arrived at my house, sent by the consulate. She'd written two postcards – one to Brian, one to me. Mine said, "I'm glad we got to visit here before there were so many hotels. No A/C." I've always been too warm-blooded. Buried beneath clothes that smelled like her and sea salt and airport fumes and absence, I found a book called *Motherless Daughters: The Legacy of Loss*. The book described the particular trauma of losing a mother at the various ages – as a child, as a teen, in the twenties, thirties, etc. The bookmark was on the page for the twenties, as if she'd left it there for me.

I sat back with the book in my hands and whispered, "Crom!"

19. Digging Postholes for Fences

BRIAN FELL IN LOVE WITH KELLEY WHEN HE SAW HER DIG-
ging postholes for a fence high in the Rocky Mountains while her
long red hair flew unbound in the alpine wind.

He told me this on the phone and asked if I wanted to go on
a hiking trip with him – just him and me.

When I got there, Kelley decided to go, too, loading up her
backpack with ours. She took us to her family's ranch land that
stretches for miles from Colorado and into Utah – thousands of
acres.

Brian went off fishing while Kelley and I sat talking around
an empty fire pit in a small canyon with a little creek and sounds
carried because the quiet was immense.

"Don't tell anyone about these drawings," she said, pointing
to the pictographs on a sandstone boulder nearby. "We don't want
anyone – the tribes or the archaeologists – to know about them. We
protect them. The tribes don't take care of things, you know," she
said all that, her long red air blowing in the wind.

We both liked political and religious topics, so we were off,
tongues running. I vaguely remembered asking Mom if she
thought that I'd like Brian's girlfriend, but I didn't remember how
she'd paused and said, "hmm."

Kelley and I had more in common than we admitted to. We
were sensitive and intense.

Brian came back with a fish, and while it smoked, the conversation did, too.

She said feminism wouldn't help women. I gave her a list of reasons for feminism, one being that rape survivors need support, not blame for no longer being virgins.

Brian said, "See, Jenny, not every woman agrees on feminism," and then walked away again up the valley.

Kelley told me she'd been raped. "Women who want the government to pay for their therapy are wasting taxpayer dollars. I never needed therapy," she said. I didn't tell her I went to therapy but paid for it myself.

"I have all I need," which led to talk about Christianity. "The first Christians were tortured for their beliefs. It's the same today. We suffer for our beliefs."

I remembered believing in my own persecution as a Christian, but the certainty no longer lived in my body.

I told her Christians had done a great deal of torturing others. I said, "Just consider Columbus. Consider the Native Americans, like the ones who lived on this land and …"

"No, Jenny." She paused, her face reddened. "No." She got up and walked away for a while into the green hills of her family's ranch and didn't say much more to me for the rest of the trip.

I sort of wished I could take it back to keep peace, but I also knew I wouldn't even if I could because peace between her and me would be impossible. I sat in silence until Brian returned with a fish. We ate and then he and I took a hike and he told me he thought he still might break up with Kelley, that he'd been thinking about it for a while, but then he'd change his mind. "She's just so Christian, and she thinks she has to save me," he said.

"Yes, she is so Christian. She can't even admit that Christians have done some torturing in the name of Christianity."

"Wow," he said, surprised.

The three of us drove back to Denver, and Kelley invited me up for dinner. She said, "I don't know how to make spaghetti vegetarian."

After too many documentaries and memories of dying deer

and chicken beheadings and dead animals by every road I'd ever driven, I'd become a vegetarian.

I told her I cooked differently for Ron, too, "I just leave the meat out of the sauce. I put it to the side, so he can mix it into the sauce if he wants."

She turned to me, angry still, or maybe angrier, and said, "Vegetarians and people like you who don't like meat are responsible for the loss of ranchers' land and livelihood."

I thought about corporations and industrialized agriculture, buying up land-use rights, wiping out family farms with their billions of dollars. Instead, I held my tongue as she said I knew nothing of ranching.

During dinner conversation, she and Brian said they'd gone to see the movie *Natural Born Killers*, but had to leave halfway through. "It was just too violent and terrible."

I said, "I can't go to movies like that. I'm such a baby. Too sensitive for the violence, but Ron went and he said that he thought it had a good message about the violent society we live in."

Kelley's face went red. "Well, I don't know what you think a good message is, but that *message* wasn't good, in my opinion."

"*I* didn't say it was a good message. *Ron* saw the movie. *He* said…"

"Yes, you did. You said it had a good message." Kelley shouted then, "We just don't agree on what *good* is."

"Kelley, I'm going outside for a minute." I got up from the table, walked out the door, went downstairs to count to ten a few dozen times. My head hurt, and I couldn't believe the conversation went that badly in so few words.

Again.

A few weeks later, Brian called me in Phoenix.

He said, "Kelley and I are getting married."

AT THE WEDDING, just two months after Mom died, Kelley didn't say a word to me. It was a traditional church wedding. She wore a family heirloom dress and a double-layer white tulle veil.

Her father invited me to help decorate the Moose Lodge for the reception. He said, "I bet you've never decorated a Moose before." I didn't tell him about the Masons and Rainbow Girls. I said, "Mancos wasn't big enough for a Moose Lodge. Grand Junction was a city to us – a place we traveled to have the goats bred, to buy peaches to freeze for the winter, for district track meets." His eyes widened a little. He handed me some crepe paper.

Brian watched while I threaded crepe paper around tables and chairs. I wanted to tell him my family secret. I'd wanted to tell him for some years and it seemed like the right time. I wore Mom's fuchsia jacket and a cowboy-themed corsage, a piece of rope shaped into the symbol for infinity given to me by one of Kelley's sisters. I told him that Mom married Dad because she was pregnant with me.

He was quiet and wore a single carnation boutonniere. "Wow," he said. He was cleaner than I'd ever seen him.

"Yeah," I said. "Mom told me never get married because you're pregnant because then you're making two mistakes instead of one."

"She said that?" He wore shiny black shoes.

"Yeah. Well, you know, it's different for women."

"Hmm." He wore a black bow tie.

I said, "I don't know why I told you this."

"I don't know either." He looked at me for a few seconds and then looked at one of his future sisters-in-law, who smiled at him. I'd given her Mom's sewing machine because I already had one and she said she her old one broke. She had three kids.

A few weeks after the wedding, Brian called from Grand Junction and said, "Kelley's pregnant."

I said, "I didn't know." And I remembered what I told him, "I didn't know! I'm so sorry."

He said, "Well, you didn't know. You were telling me about yourself."

We sat in silence. I had damaged us. We had lost something we'd never get back.

"I wanted to marry Kelley. I really love her, and I was going to marry her anyway."

"I know, Brian. That's good."

During their wedding I had heard one of the sisters say, "Wow, Kelley's really curvy. I never noticed that." When I remembered that now, I knew why Mom had said that Brian would make a good father.

She knew Kelley was pregnant and that she would have the baby, that Brian would marry her, that life would change for us all, and that Kelley and I would probably not get along.

Mom had left debt, as promised – a lot of it on credit cards, but I dealt with that when creditors called. I said, "She died." Every one of them hung up, saying, "Sorry for your loss," after asking if I could pay her debt. I told them I had enough of my own debt.

A nice man from the state of Colorado and another nice man from the life insurance company gave Brian and me money.

I used that money to visit relatives.

I visited Brian and Kelley and their infant son, Paden, a smaller version of Brian – perfect and mighty. I sent little things – a baby spoon, spill-proof cups, a baby nail clipper, until Brian told me to stop. Financial abundance was the only way I could connect with them, but they didn't want that either.

Ron, Chiara, and I visited Uncle John and Aunt Barb in Minnesota, and Chiara and I went to their youngest son's wedding. Much was made of the bride's tiny waist. Uncle John and Uncle Wils, the rich uncle, leaned together across the table from us and said, "Did you feel it?" and made moaning sounds – sexual noises. They put their hands around an imaginary tiny waist.

Then Kelley had another son thirteen months after the first son. Wyatt, cut from the same cloth as Chiara, blond, blue-eyed and looked like me and my father. She said she wanted them to be close in age so they'd have a close relationship like Brian and I had. She believed it was our eighteen months apart that made us wander together in wide open fields and whisper together in the dark.

Ron and I had a couple of Thanksgivings with Brian because Mom was gone, and because I wanted a Colorado Thanksgiving. There were dozens of children in each generation of Brian's new family.

With so many children, education was a popular topic. Things that were said were things I'd left behind, ideas I no longer shared.

The sister who was a Grand Junction teacher said, "You can't do anything with the kids nowadays to make them behave. You're not allowed to hit 'em." I remembered the principal, Mr. Culp, and I knew Colorado was still a corporal punishment state. She said, "Of course, you only hit kids if you love them."

Kelley's mother talked about the English-only campaign of the day and didn't want Spanish spoken in schools, "Nobody speaks Spanish in Colorado, anyway," she said. I wondered if Mom had ever told her what she did for a living. I wondered if she knew Colorado was a Spanish word.

Brian and Kelley both said they'd left college because of the liberal education system. They'd find a way to get a Christian education.

The family talked about the people who worked ranches – the harsh conditions of the work and life. Kelley said, "They're citizens and have a choice, but they live out there, most of the time. They could live anywhere, but a lot of Mexicans choose to live that way."

I said, "You mean Americans, right? Citizens?"

Brian and Kelley laughed, "Yeah. So, the Americans..." and couldn't finish what they were saying because they were laughing.

One of the mothers said, "I want that bumper sticker 'AIDS makes vegetables out of fruits.'" They all laughed while Ron and I sat horrified and angry and speechless.

Kelley said, "They're always talking about getting special rights, but everyone should have the same rights."

Kelley's mother said, "Dick won't go to San Francisco unless I walk behind him." Kelley's father laughed.

When children got out of line, we heard, "Do you want a spanking?" followed by approval, "You're a good parent. You've got to raise kids with discipline."

They talked about being pro-life but had the Second Amendment in calligraphy on the wall.

During one argument, Kelley supported an assertion by telling me to read my mother's Bible. What could Kelley have possibly known of my mother's Bible?

We didn't have Thanksgiving with them again. They never invited us. I don't know if we would've gone.

Brian and I didn't talk much after that. He was born again as a Baptist, and I no longer believed in penitence or in following the rules the way he did.

I told Brian I'd like to visit, but he said not to.

He said, "I told Kelley something about you so she'd understand how you are."

"What did you tell her?"

"I told her why you're the way you are. A feminist."

I wanted to give him a list of my reasons, but I knew the reason he meant.

"I had to tell her," he said. "You cause problems between us. I lose my temper."

"So you told her I had an abortion because I create problems between you and make you lose your temper."

"It didn't work out the way I thought it would."

We used to trust each other with our sins and fears and our anger, talking in the dark while Jesus sat on the trailer roof. We whispered because God always listened and we wanted to keep our confidences to ourselves.

But Kelley's God heard all thoughts, humans could hold no confidences from Him. She once told me, "There's no such thing as personal privacy – that's a human idea, a feminist idea. Our parents opened our mail. I'll open my kids' mail, too. There should never be secrets from family."

But I caused problems for them, so I did as the preacher at

Kelley and Brian's wedding asked. He said to the congregation, "Will you promise to support these two in marriage?" and we did. All of us. Even me.

Brian re-enlisted in the army at the age of thirty-five, when those twin towers were felled. He had to go through basic training again.

"It was easier this time around," he wrote in a letter.

He shipped off to Iraq – a second time, having gone the first time when Colin Powell pulled the forces back. Brian wrote letters to me – he wrote, "one of the thermometers hit 142 degrees," and he said they were making things safer by taking guns out of Iraqi homes. He wrote about saving a woman from being attacked by a group of men, and saving another soldier's life and praying with him beside a jeep tire under a nimbus of enemy fire. He used a pejorative to refer to Iraqi people, and when I wrote to him that I would've thought professional soldiers would try to be more PC, he wrote, "What's PC mean? Personally Citified? Perfectionist Constantly? Porcelain Courage?"

Brian wrote that the whole culture was oppressive. "Women in America don't understand how bad things can be and how lucky they are."

I called Kelley because I thought I should. I swore to myself I wouldn't say something terrible to her, something she didn't need. She was losing her hair. "I'm so worried, but I believe in what we're doing. I support our troops, the soldiers keeping us safe, fighting for our freedom. Paden helps me so much. He's five and he can cook and clean. He's my little man."

She'd placed a miniature American flag in the flower well of Mom's gravestone.

I heard the boys in the background, quietly playing. Legos and the soft conversation of little boys. I imagined them as soldiers, then closed my mind to the thought of it.

"Muslim is an evil religion. We've gotta take care of them once and for all," she said.

And my mouth unhinged, "The religion is called Islam. Followers are Muslims."

"Jenny. Just. Stop."

Kelley didn't allow that my connection to my brother had, in great part, been affected by war, too – even before he knew her, I was there, wanting more for him and something other than violence for everyone else. I never had any other way to deal with it than to learn more, to be some kind of know-it-all, to try to fix things through more information, more understanding.

Connections to them and to other family members stretched and snapped the farther I got from where I'd come: an American flag waving from the bracket by the trailer door and ranchers and Mormons and Masons and a Christianity based in western pioneer mythology and guns under the bed. These severings included my father. He and his wife sold their house in California and took their collection of expensive musical instruments with them when they bought ninety acres in Arkansas. He said, "The people here say we fit right in."

He called several months after Mom died and said he'd had a scare with his heart. Nothing to worry about. Doctors said he was strong as an ox, but he'd had a scare. Wanted us to know. Then he started telling stories, thought I should know something about my mother. A secret I didn't know, he told me, to better understand her and things that happened.

"I met your mother in a bar. She was drunk and spitting ice chips at the bartender and then at me."

"And then you had to marry her because she was pregnant with me."

He was surprised that I knew. He said, "Well, now. That's. Um. That's not why. I would've married her anyway."

I offered him silence. I hadn't known about the ice chips.

He said, "I really loved her."

"Hmm," I said. "Goodbye, Dad."

What I didn't say was *Thank you for this great gift*.

He gave me a memory of my mother not having to take care

of anyone but herself, a memory when she was full of herself, and her dreams were a living, drunk, and youthful thing, a memory of her spitting ice chips at this man in a deep snowy valley with a midnight blue and star-scattered sky.

20. A Wide River

MOM'S DYING MADE ME AWARE THAT I DIDN'T WANT TO die in the paved desert of ever more houses and golf courses and water fountains. Chiara was almost two and got a fever on a 122-degree day, the fire ants lived in the grass where she played, and she could only use the slide at the playground for a few months of the year without getting burned.

Ron wanted to move back to Oregon – he'd lived there for a couple of years as a teenager. I wanted to go home to Colorado, but the Silicon Forest in the Pacific Northwest saw its boom time. So Ron and I moved even farther from family.

"My truck needs an oil change, love," I said. "It's been a while," as I stirred pasta in our Beaverton, Oregon, apartment with the rectangular kitchen and a garden window, where two cats sat swishing their tails at house sparrows.

"I'll take care of it," he said, clicking the mouse, playing his first-person shooter video game.

"Well, you're busy. I could take it to someone."

"No. I don't want some guy to rip you off. I'll do it. I promise."

We had this conversation several times, as he walked out the door to work, as we assembled a playhouse in Chiara's room.

Then, as I took a left from Murray onto Allen, I heard a boom – an explosion, really, and the truck stopped. No power steering, no sound, no lights. Burned oil. Two men pushed me in to the gas station.

One of the men opened the hood and said, "No oil. Totaled.

If this were a horse, I'd put a bullet in her." I burst into tears, then he slipped away, drove away in his Ford F-150.

The gray dark of Oregon took getting used to after the sun of Colorado and Arizona. I hadn't adjusted.

Ron ran multiple computers. He connected computers to the virtual geography of the now expanding Internet to serve up webpages and manage email on multiple domains and to play computer games. He was a programmer creating electronic design automation software that electronic engineers used to design schematics and circuit boards. He left the computers on full time, saying, "It takes more energy to turn them back on again."

But we were going to be eco-friendly in Oregon because isn't that what you do when you move to Oregon? I had the lights on mid-afternoon when he came home one day. He said, "You're using electricity," and reached over, flipped the switch.

I'd have to get used to the rain, the gray, the close-in sky.

Ron and I would have to navigate the messages in our heads, the stories of money our families told – his mother's childhood of newspaper in shoes in Indiana, and my mother's broke times and skier dreams, his mother's saying "We'll see," and my mother's "There's no way" and her crying.

We'd navigate Ron's having lived in a house with a mortgage and having a loving step-father, a long haul truck driver, and spending nights with his brother in the dark of the closed truck trailer on cross-country trucking trips. We'd navigate his mother the bank teller and clerk at Walmart. We'd be surrounded by the ghosts of our forefathers' insistence that life had been difficult and they'd pulled up their bootstraps to make it better for us.

We'd navigate our better angels with the wider perspective that all is not as it appears to be and mythologies are created and that everything can be rewritten and is.

We'd navigate everyone else and their "Yeah, that's nothing" and "You should've grown up in my house" and truth and lies in stories about money and love and difficulty and yet we'd cling to the commitments we'd make and the dreams we'd have.

We'd navigate the truth that we'd never suffered like so many had suffered even in our worst times.

We'd navigate a wide river.

Ron would have work, make good money, and have insurance for us all. I'd have to come to some terms with myself – what could I earn? How could I be mother, employee, wife, citizen, feminist? I knew I'd be damned if I did and damned if I didn't, so what would I do, having learned that from my mother? I wanted to be a teacher, having been inspired by Mom's work in the world and despite remembering her saying, "Don't be a teacher. Be anything but a teacher." I went back to college, child in tow to become a teacher.

When Chiara was born, I wanted to cook family meals, to abide that tradition Mom had.

For years, I cooked three different meals. A sample night: salad with vegetarian sausage covered in blue cheese dressing for me; macaroni and cheese with a little side salad, no dressing, for Chiara; red sauce pasta with hamburger for Ron.

Ron said, "Vegetables stunt your growth." Funny because of his 6'4" height. Ron had learned to make macaroni and cheese when he was seven because his mom said, "You'll eat what I cook or you'll cook for yourself."

My battle with food expanded along with my expanding middle.

We ate at different times as the years passed, and after a while I gave up my vegetarianism. I gave up carb-heavy foods like bread and pasta, lost twenty pounds. Had a breast reduction, lost ten more.

Then I gained it back because I love bagels, gorgonzola cheese, and red wine. Pie.

When we first got married, I left his socks where he flung them, and I didn't want to have to ask him to pick them up. The relationship magazines said it was my problem if either of those bothered me.

I wrote in my journals over the years, "Be of service" and "I want more," pondering the contradictions.

I USED THE rest of the insurance money and PERS money from Mom's death to pay for graduate school and to make a small down payment on a house in Portland, where we had two dogs, some cats, some chickens in the backyard, and grew kale and planted forget-me-nots and watched the rain under the streetlamps. We watched Mount St. Helens, called *Loowit* by the Native Americans, smoking from time to time and watched the fireworks at Fort Vancouver from the upstairs window while the dogs trembled. We drove to eastern Oregon to look at a sky full of stars with telescopes Ron made by hand, and a whole childhood passed through it all. We hugged some mighty trees.

Brian and I raised our children separately in an attempt to minimize each other's influence on our children. I know he'll argue that. But it's the basic truth of it.

Brian's sons were raised with firearms the way Brian and I had been. Ron and I decided not to have a gun in our house, but we made sure Chiara had a good pocket knife.

Still, our children had much in common – they were children of nature but were wary of water. Paden nearly drowned and had to be revived just as he finished his first year of life. I heard about it later, as an aside. "Oh, I should tell you," Brian said. Chiara knows what happened to her grandmother and her cousin and rebelled at swimming lessons.

Now the three children are grown.

CHIARA CAME HOME from college her freshman year and we got chili cheese fries from Burgerville and sat on her bed watching the rain in the streetlamp. I told her about my writing and the literary reading series I started for women. She explained to me the phrase "gender binary" and "tone policing" and the evolving academic and practical language of feminism and social justice. The river widened.

She hiked part of El Camino de Santiago in Spain during a winter break. She sent me a birthday card and included a rosary in the envelope, significant because I'd exposed her to a patchwork mythology of paganism and Goddess-worship and nonreligious ideas and antireligious rebellion and the thought that global religions have something and nothing to offer. I'd warned her about Mormon missionaries. "They're after your uterus," I said. But there in Spain in an old cathedral, candle-lit and incense-filled, she'd found something holy. She dipped the rosary in holy water, sat in the pews, and wished a wish for me in each bead, and blessed it in the water again. The rosary fell out of the envelope; there were marks in the card – round indentations, longer dents as it was pushed through the mail machinery. I told myself that someone found it who needed it because sometimes we need a story.

Chiara is a scientist, a doctoral candidate at the University of Colorado Boulder. She studies the effects of global warming on high-altitude species – her workplace is filled with marmot, fox, deer, and bear, not far from where her grandmother is buried.

Before she left, she threw out her childhood rock collections and drawings and bird feathers hanging on fishing wire in the window and photos tacked to the wall. She threw away her journals – I hoped I wasn't the reason she did that. I promised I wouldn't read them if she wanted to keep them. She shook her head. They're gone. I cried when I put them in the trash. I worry about her memories being lost with the writing.

She packed her belongings and put her bike on top of the Prius that had belonged to Ron.

She said, "Do you think I have too much stuff? Is this too much?"

I peered into her car and said, "Everything you own fits into one small car with room to spare."

She smiled and hugged me. I took a photo of her in front of the house with the sunburst front porch, the new drought-resistant plants, the mature fruit trees, the lilacs long past the seasons of being purple.

I love you. So proud. Thank you for everything. I'll see you soon. Don't worry. Be careful. I mean it, be really careful. I love you.

And off she drove.

I breathed the go-away-pain breath.

Wyatt is mathematically minded, though I don't know him much more than that. I didn't want to be the aunt on the phone having those awkward conversations, so I sent gift cards on birthdays.

Paden is an Army Ranger. Brian sent a photo of him holding a small, dead shark with the caption, "This is what rangers do for fun." I didn't answer.

Brian and I had both returned with our children to Mancos as tourists when Kelley and the boys had some spicy southwest Colorado food and got sick. Brian ate the same food but didn't get sick. Brian said, "I guess you have to have a certain kind of stomach like you and I have from growing up in Mancos."

I took pictures of Chiara, the mountains and memory in the background. She rode thousands of miles in the car during her childhood, never asking "Are we there yet?"

Another time, I returned, alone, searching for an ending to this book, just after a near-evacuation due to the threat of wildfire. A woman in one of the four art galleries said, "No one had to be evacuated after all – we were very lucky."

Another woman recognized me because she'd worked at the restaurant with my mom. She said my high school track records stood for thirty years and had just been broken the previous spring. She said they might not have changed them yet, that I should check to see if they were still up. I went to the gym to take a picture. She said the gym was open because of the evacuation, but nobody would be there.

Outside the gym, a dozen tents were set up. The nearby reservation had been evacuated.

I walked into the sweat- and sage-scented gym, saw the collection of sports team banners, a couple with my name on them. A young woman wearing an orange vest came over, said hello, and

I told her why I was there. She said, "Oh, cool. Go ahead," and I walked into the gym. A group of young people – Native Americans, mostly, sat on benches, some with orange vests. A couple of young men played basketball, shoes squeaking, laughter, the breath and grunt and push of competition.

We talked about sports, but none of them had played in this gym. The sports leagues had changed – it had been one of the last connections between the nearby reservations and the larger Mancos community.

The young people watching over things were too young for me to know, but we talked about the fire and basketball – our greatest victories and defeats. When I said my track records had just been taken down, I got high-fives.

We all cried when one of the young men talked about the best shot he ever missed – the beauty of utter failure in his telling.

It rained when I was there, and I took credit for it because even when I left Portland it rained on me. It wasn't the usual Colorado sky. The sky was soot and gray. There was the smell of ash and sage and rain.

The mother of one of my former classmates was working at the gas station. While she rang up my gas purchase, she frowned and said, "The town's changed." Her son's truck was parked outside with a bumper sticker that said, "You find it offensive, I find it funny," and another one that said, "To Conquer a Nation, First Disarm its Citizens."

I saw a business flyer in a café. Mean Ranch Daughter Patty, who told me I didn't belong, was selling real estate.

A woman at another art gallery said Fern Ellis wrote a book containing the names of all the people who'd ever lived in Mancos – our names weren't there. Paul's family wasn't included, even though his generation was the third to live in Mancos. Hugh (Huey) Whiteskunk's name was missing.

BRIAN AND I text from time to time, trying as our mother would wish for us to "Work it out."

He and Kelley sold the land they'd owned on the Front Range and bought a big truck and trailer that will be their home. They're going to do a travel ministry. He asked after Ron's parents.

He texted, "Didn't Joe and Sue do a traveling ministry at one time? We'd love to see them."

Ron shook his head when I told him. He went for a long bike ride.

As Brian and Kelley are leaving Colorado, I want to return – not to Mancos, not to the Front Range, probably, but somewhere in Colorado.

I remembered the moment in the Denver airport thinking that my leaving could be permanent.

I texted, "I want to come back to Colorado."

He typed, "Colorado's going up in pot smoke. You can have it."

Epilogue

MY EXTENDED FAMILY RELATIONSHIPS ARE DOTS AND lines from Minnesota to Colorado to Arizona, time and emotion and distance. I've been unable to navigate that landscape. I chose a different geography.

And I wrote.

I wrote against the loneliness of three people becoming one each. I wrote about the high desert and the mountains and alpine meadows while I listened to the rain and drank coffee and lived among wide rivers and Douglas-fir and hawthorn trees. I wrote about motherhood and not spanking and trying not to yell. I wrote bigger things about being free and saying no and about god as something other than stained glass, robe-shrouded men, sin listing, and forgiveness on knees. I wrote about the matriarchy Mom whispered in my ear in the red dust about being in charge of the food source, seeking other gods, and then seeking nothing and untying the knots in my mind, pulling out poetic threads, removing what wasn't needed.

I wrote regret and sculpted a narrative where I didn't talk too much, and I didn't tell sad stories.

It's a painful thing to claim who we are, who we've been and failed to be, but when we do the things that separate us can be faced. We can begin again.

While I was visiting Chiara in Colorado, where she planted grasses among the aspen trees and in fields above 9,000 feet, a man told me he had a buddy who was "cleaning up Minturn." The farm we lived on outside of Minturn, those two acres, had been a plant nursery when Mom died and was now, after twenty years, a dump for cars. The man said, "My buddy's getting rid of all those terrible trailers, you know."

I said, "I grew up in a trailer." It was enough for him to understand.

But so often I can't find the words that change things and that say what I mean to say. I'm ever counting to ten–words spoken are tricky things.

Chiara once asked me about something Kelley had said to her on the phone. Kelley told Chiara that her Uncle Brian was fighting for her freedom. "What does she mean by 'Freedom isn't free, Mama?'"

I told her that's a hard question because I'd answer it differently than Kelley would. I used to know how Kelley would answer it, but I'd forgotten that way of thinking, having wandered for so long. I no longer knew the way through that landscape.

I lived in a new place now that healed the wounds of my upbringing–small and massive, imagined and real, the things I've done and felt couldn't be contained within the old terrain.

That place was a time before the Pacific Northwest and plentiful rain, where still-erupting volcanoes are called mountains and old-growth trees have lulled us into a feeling of permanence. Vast is too small a word for the fjords of the Olympic Peninsula, the valleys of vineyards formed by relentless floods, and the Columbia River Gorge with its waterfalls. Deep forests, wide rivers, creeks the size of Colorado rivers, and the ocean are my kind of wilderness.

The Pacific Ocean pushes up against land, and everything shifts, impermanent, but at the same time continuous. The water my mother breathed in her last breaths could be the water at my feet on an Oregon shore. The cycle is constantly connecting the ocean and all things, resting sometimes in a heart-shaped agate or a universe of living and dying in a tide pool or in a bird bone sunning on a beach after its journeys.

The source of this wildness, the waves, the fire and stone, is so much chaos and chance, but also patterns and predictability of injustice and change and love, another too-small word for its depth and breadth.

I used to have a different mind and soul. I regret many things. I write to let them go and also to remember, to make sure my compass includes the geography that's not just where I stand, but also beyond me.

I wrote my mother's forgiveness into the lines and acceptance as a whisper between them.

I wrote myself resilient.

I wrote about revolutions, inner and outer, and about sex and being a woman and about grief and never being quite good enough and about being something more.

Portland's nearness to the Pacific Ocean offered a new landscape, and I tried to become worthy of it: expansive, nurturing the rich inner life beneath.

In my artist's mind, I sat at the table of my childhood, where I wrote across the table from an army recruiter and ephemeral peaches and haunting deer souls with my pen, carving out words and ideas, seeking a different path than my brother's.

The pen wrote truth into the steam of truck windows. I looked through it from outside in and inside out and remembered. I spent a lot of time alone with my thoughts. I'd grown up as one child of two in a deep valley. The pen gave me company and solitude. I was grateful.

I wrote to change my relationship to my brother, and I wrote to change him, too.

He's read these words and said, "I remember that, too" and "Nobody's perfect" and "When you point your finger at someone, there are always three pointing back at you."

He's said, "We didn't mean to leave you out."

But that's been our conflict. I want out.

I no longer believe in redemption: no human aggression

can be paid in full or compensated. There's no reason good enough for the terrible events of time.

The valley of my youth is filling with concrete and golf courses, and when I visited I didn't know where I was, the landmarks. One of the ghost towns, once consisting almost entirely of Latino families, is going to be made into a golf course and resort of red quartzite and aspens and glacial peaks.

Uncle John wrote a book, too. He said, "I got to a point where I couldn't do anything, so I sat at the typewriter until I got it all out of me." He wrote Vietnam and grief until he could stand again. He and his son marched in a gay rights parade together by the Mississippi River.

During the years of writing, other writers have said, "We're all unprepared for college," so I rewrote scenes showing Mr. Adcock throwing blocks of wood at us in shop and Mr. Russell throwing erasers in science to clarify the metaphor.

"You'll have to explain things a bit here because people nowadays will think this is all archaic" was a note I got on my writing about Mancos and those years as a teenager, struggling with my body, my sexuality, and spiritual loss. I rewrote.

Other writers said, "This is a story about small-town people." They wrote in the margins of my manuscripts that these were outdated phrases: "Boys will be boys" and "The Indians today aren't the same Indians of old." They said dogs on chains and near worship of the Second Amendment were limited to, and certainties for, only ignorant small-town folk, so I rewrote.

When people said they saw Jesus as a mere peacemaker, a gentle god, I rewrote.

I would be precise, I thought, and kept writing until any reader of this memoir, this piece of art, this ambition would understand the metaphors and the urgency.

I'm all the characters in this narrative, symbolically, metaphorically – to someone somewhere.

Should I have known or been better? Can I be? Will I be?

I'm both haunted and comforted by my mother's ghost. I

ask her, "Who was the first person you saw when you died?" and "What do you know now that you didn't know then?" and "Will we always be sad if we were sad in this life?"

Whatever holds our grief is massive. It's big enough and wide enough to hold the ocean. This is why I'm here writing and pacing and doing. I'm trying to build something big enough to contain it.

Mom told us we could do anything we put our minds to, and I put my mind to this.

And with my pen, I write the houses and hotels back into being bobcats and wild streams and magpies. I write the elk enough space and the mountain lions and bighorn sheep return and the forests grow thick and the grasslands and great herds return and all the missing people rise and some disappear, as I will in time.

And things are as they should be again. It is all becoming winding alpine rivers and aspen leaves quaking and oceans void of warships. It is all too much for words and is countless and wild.

Acknowledgements

THANK YOU TO ARIEL GORE, YOU'RE THE BEST CITY GIRL a person could know. Thank you for teaching me the most important writing rules. Everyone should take your classes and buy all your books.

Thank you to the Wayward Writers in The Literary Kitchen, too numerous to name with a collective skillset that is wondrous and mighty. I wouldn't have written the book without your support. I can't name everyone, but you're here, ye Waywards. Special thanks to Margaret Elysia Garcia, Jenny Hayes, Sarah Maria Medina, Michelle Gonzales, Ky Delaney, Hyla, Rocky Hatley, Bonnie Ditlevsen, Mai'a Williams, China Martins, Vanessa Deza-Hangad, Rebeca Dunn-Krahn, Jo Penney, Cayena Bravia, Meg Weber. Go to *www.literarykitchen.com* to see books by other Lit Kit authors.

Thank you for all kinds of things: Charlotte DeKanter Chung, Sara Jeanne, Rebecca Fish-Ewen, Jenna Powers-Fox, Monica Drake, Ellen Urbani, Janet Jackson, Kerri O'Boyle, Lisa Galloway, Nina Rockwell, Shannon Barber, Rene Denfeld, Sue Parker, Cheri Cooper Clark, Craig Ottinger, Lori Walker, Corie Skolnick, Kate Carroll de Gutes, Kirsten Larson, Zach Ellis, Gloria Harrison, Amber Keller, Jen Violi, Mari Shepard-Glenn, Gigi Little, Andrew Gurevich, Celeste Gurevich, Sarah Hart, Brenda Taulbee, Jamondria Marnice Harris, S. Renee Mitchell, Leigh Anne Kranz.

Thanks to Nina Packebush for being my query buddy. Ugh! You are so funny and the best kind of buddy in times of crisis. Someone will publish your YA novel soon.

Thank you, other great teachers: Rosebud Ben-Oni, Jessica Morrell, Patricia Louise MacAodha, Lidia Yuknavitch.

Thanks to Mark Russell and Lasara Fox Allen for early reviews.

Thanks to Ander Monson, Peter Mountford, Victor LaValle, Matthew Simmons, Kevin Sampsell for extending a hand at just the right moment.

Thanks to The Attic, Tin House, The Literary Kitchen, Willamette Writers, Oregon Writers Colony, and Corporeal Writers for the service you provide to writers and their readers and to me.

Thanks to the students of Hillsboro Public Schools, Portland Public Schools, especially the Metropolitan Learning Center, and thanks to the students of Village Home for teaching me.

I'm grateful to RV Branham and MF McCauliff, Carrie Seitzinger and Matty Byloos, Kelli Martinelli, Carissa Miller, Ann Imig, and Kristi DiLallo. Portions and likenesses of portions of this memoir have been published in *Monkey Puzzle Press*, *Gobshite Quarterly*, *Nailed* Magazine, *Hip Mama*, *The Literary Kitchen*, *Seattle City Arts* Magazine, *Solstice* Magazine, and *Columbia Review*.

Thanks to Davis Slater, Domi Shoemaker, Robert Duncan Gray, Nancy Slavins, Josh Lubin, Kevin Sampsell, Melissa Dodson, Carrie Seitzinger, the people of The Pointy House, Olivia Olivia, Curtis Whitecarroll, Amanda Helstrom-White, Sam Snoek-Brown, Sally Lehman, Jessica Ann, A.M. O'Malley, and more for inviting me to read at the your shindigs.

Thanks for writing with me and for the therapy ("friendapy") sessions: Dot Hearn, Deb Scott, Jamalieh Haley, Mo Daviau, Kate Dreyfus, Cooper Lee Bombardier, Laura Green, and Anna Doogan.

Thanks to all the Unchaste Readers (*www.unchastereaders.com*) of the reading series with the same name for all your generosity and support and survival and art and for creating the series with me. Thanks to Dena Rash Guzman.

Thanks to Jaquira Diaz for making me think at least twice about every word. Kate Dreyfus, thank you for your sensitivity.

Ijeoma Oluo, thank you, for the sensitivity reading and for everything else. All offenses are my own.

Rhonda Hughes, thank you. I had a manuscript I liked, but I could only take it to a certain level. You made it so much better. To edit is Truly Divine.

Scott Parker, thank you for putting your mind to this text. It would not be the same without you.

Adam McIsaac, thank you for the cover that was so perfect I thought I'd seen it before – a cover that had always been the cover.

Brian, thanks for the most excellent ending to this book. Write your own book. I'll read it. I didn't sneeze in your cereal on purpose. It was an accident. I wish you'd believe that.

Thanks to Judy Marshall for being all that you were and all that you've become. It will be good to see you again someday – way down the road.

Thank you, Ron. I love you so much. Thanks for the Salt River and for all the ice cream and for listening to my stories over and over. Thank you for Enough.

Thank you, Chiara, for knowing me so well and loving me so fiercely. Thank you for putting up with dashboard burritos and miles and miles and miles in the car. When you think of the landscape of your childhood, I hope it's vast. I tried. You were amazing. So proud.

If I didn't name you, it's not because I forgot you. You're here. Right here. Thank YOU so much! For a long list of people I'm grateful to: *www.jennyforrester.com*.

Thank you, everyone, for Our Book. It took us a lifetime, but we did it.

Love,
Jenny